FEET FIRST AGAIN

THE AUTHOR

FEET FIRST AGAIN

By

STANLEY MATTHEWS

(Blackpool and England)

NICHOLAS KAYE
LONDON

First published by
Nicholas Kaye & Co.
1 Trebeck Street, London, W.1
1952

TO BETTY, JEAN AND STANLEY JUNIOR

Printed for Nicholas Kaye & Co., at the St. Ann's Press, Park Road, Altrincham, and entirely produced in Great Britain

CONTENTS

LIST OF ILLUSTRATIONS

FOREWORD

by Frank Butler

I AM particularly delighted to write the foreword to *Feet First Again* because when I supplied a few words to the original book *Feet First* more than four years ago I believed in my heart that by the 1952–53 season the great Stanley Matthews would have retired from top-class football. I was prepared to see him sitting back, cherished by millions of fans as the greatest player of this generation —and possibly of any generation.

But Stanley Matthews, approaching thirty-seven, is as fit as he was at seventeen, which is a great tribute to his way of living and training. That old Black Magic is still in his feet, and last season I saw him playing as well as ever, bamboozling three young players, and bringing roars of delight from opposing supporters. Yes, everybody in football is a Matthews fan—even frustrated home supporters when he visits their ground. I am convinced he will still be fooling defences at forty.

Matthews is not only the finest footballer it has been my privilege to watch, but he is one of the most charming and likeable men in sport. He has never worn a hat in his life, but had he done so at no time in twenty-two wonderful years would he have required a larger size.

It is an understatement merely to say Stanley Matthews is the most modest of all the great princes of sport. I have seen him perform in many parts of the world, and he is always the same unassuming fellow who tucks himself into a corner seat in some hotel on the eve of an international, leaving all the limelight to those who wish to seek it. Although he has broken all international records, having made 63 appearances for England, and once for Great Britain, he is as unsophisticated as the day he first played for England when only nineteen.

I still have not seen Stanley commit the mildest foul, and know that, even if he goes on playing in League football until he is fifty, I never shall, because Stanley Matthews hasn't yet learned after nearly a quarter of a century playing football how to foul. Just as he never has an unkind word to say against any opponent—and in his long career I have seen perplexed backs treat him anything but kindly when they realize his skill is something out of this world.

A long time ago I dubbed Matthews "The Wizard of Dribble." This title is now frequently used. Matthews is more than a wizard, he is a football phenomenon. We should cherish him because I am more convinced than ever that when the sad day comes for him to put away his boots and jersey for the last time, we shall not in our life-time see such natural ability, such ball-control and such fantastic and fascinating dribbling. Something will go out of Soccer the day Matthews retires.

Every plot and counter-plot discussed in the past two decades to find the way of playing Matthews has been wasted. When Stanley is in top form, he is unplayable. The back who is told to beat him with first-time tackling is made to look ridiculous; the defender who stands away is left appearing equally foolish by the maestro's magic. There doesn't seem to be a solution to his two-way swerve and twinkling toes. The only way to stop Matthews is to prevent the ball reaching him, but while that is a cast-iron theory, it is not an easy one to bring into practice.

Above all this, Matthews stands out as Soccer's No. 1 gentleman on and off the field. He has been a credit to England, Stoke City and Blackpool for a long, long time. With normal luck and health, he will continue to serve football for some seasons to come.

August, 1952.

CHAPTER I

BY SPECIAL REQUEST

I look forward to another five years in football . . . . Crazy Transfer Fee reaches £34,000. . . . Austrians, Brazilians, Uruguayans, and Russians will take some holding . . . . The Bogota Business was like an eight day's wonder. . . . Still chasing a Cup Winner's Medal. . . " Who do you think you are—' Fanny ' Walden? " . . . I try a new trick but end in a stew.

WHEN some years ago I sat down to put the pieces together to what I hoped would be an interesting story, I never thought I should four years later be asked to sit down again to revise and add later exploits to my memoirs. But that is exactly what has happened, and I am happy if only to know that a footballer's life is of sufficient interest to cause such a request to be made.

I was sincere when I wrote four years ago that I reckoned I had another five years in first-class football. Well, I have been fortunate enough to survive four years, and have one more to go, but I feel so fit and strong to-day that in all sincerity I do believe I still have another five years to go in League football—always providing I have my fair share of good luck.

Many things have happened in the past four years. Players have been transferred I discussed how transfer fees had gone up and up until Sunderland had paid £20,050 to Newcastle United for Len Shackleton. Well, since then, transfer fees have rocketed to even more fantastic heights. A couple of score of players have been transferred for £20,000 or more, while the record stands at the £34,000 Sheffield Wednesday paid Notts County for Jackie Sewell.

England played in the World Cup for the first time in Rio in 1950. I travelled through Canada with the F.A. team. Argentina visited London for the first time. The foreign challenge has increased, and we know that the Austrians, the Brazilians and the holders of the World Cup—the Uruguayans—as well as the Russians are going to take some holding, although I believe that the rest of the world will continue to find there is still plenty of swish left in the old Lion's tail.

The Bogota Business has come and gone like an eight day's wonder, but there is not any doubting that when the first threat came in the spring and summer of 1950, and the professional clubs from Colombia were enticing our star players with attractive contracts to fly away to South America, the English League clubs were alarmed.

I have also played in a second Cup Final, although that elusive Cup Winner's Medal continues to escape me, because, as against Manchester United in the 1947–48 season, Blackpool again missed the boat against Newcastle United at Wembley in 1950–51.

These, and many other stories, I have put to paper. I think my story is now a better one. I hope you share my opinion. Certainly, I am grateful that I never started this book in 1939 as I had intended. It was my father who subdued my youthful ambitions to become an author. I had hoped at the time he would encourage me when I told him my plans, but his dry reply "Who do you think you are —Fanny Walden?" made me feel very humble. And so I accepted his sound advice to wait until I had really lived, and had a story worth telling that would be of some interest to the community. I realized the fact that having played seventeen times for England at twenty-three was, after all, not so very important. Dad was the wise man of our family, and if any of us were entitled to claim a story that would make interesting reading it was dad. To most folk he was plain Jack Matthews, the modest grey-haired little man who owned the barber's shop at Number 7, Market Street, Hanley, but old-timers would address him with the air of folk proud to be familiar with a celebrity. They remembered him as Jack Matthews, the "Fighting Barber from Hanley," who as a featherweight boxer had taken part in 350 fights—including some thrilling bouts at the old National Sporting Club in Covent Garden, London.

Dad was too modest to believe that his successes and failures would interest anyone outside his own family. In fact, it was difficult for any member of our family to get him to talk about himself.

The war has come and gone, and I have mellowed with the years between. I am not old at thirty-six, but I hope that a few of the events in my career will be of some interest to those who love the game. At least I am satisfied in my own mind that it is a more readable story than it would have been if written impulsively in 1939. I could have waited until I had enjoyed a fuller life with richer experiences, but as I have experienced may happy hours in the service of football I have set myself to the task of relating how it all began while my memory is still green.

I have only one regret my story has been delayed. It will not be read by my father, who did on January 17, 1945.

From my earliest childhood I was "mad" about football, and much of the time I should have devoted to studying was spent clock-gazing at Wellington Road School, Hanley. As soon as the four o'clock bell rang my books were thrown into my desk, and I was homeward bound with a brick or paper ball at my toes. Tea was a meal that only brought anxiety for my mother as I stoked away slices of bread and jam, washed down by cups of tea. Then off like a March hare to the strip of waste land opposite our house which in those days meant more to me than Wembley or Hampden Park.

The local kids got together for a match every evening while the light lasted. These strange games were fought with more determination than is often put into a Cup Final or an international match. Only the very young can appreciate such enthusiasm. Sometimes we had twenty a side, but on evenings when the weather forced many of the mothers to keep their young sons indoors—at the risk of mutiny—we were content to play with half-a-dozen of the all-weather regulars.

My older brothers, Jack and Arthur, played football, but preferred athletics and boxing. Both were fine sprinters, and frequently brought home medals after athletic meetings. Jack, the oldest member of the family, was also a good boxer, and I watched several of his fights at the Palais de Danse in Hanley.

But back to my calf days. When our pitch was water-logged, as it so often was during the winter, I would amuse myself for hours kicking a rubber ball against our garden wall. Mother often despaired, declaring she could not understand how I could waste so many hours when I might be doing something that might be useful to me in later years.

Mother was quite right in feeling I was an idler, but I am certain my ball-control can be traced back to a small rubber ball and a garden wall. As the years rolled by I found I could use a ball more or less how I liked, and even Arthur, who looked upon me as a nuisance, used to say I had trained the ball to obey me.

But one day my tricks caused trouble. I had been trying for weeks to lift the ball over two kitchen chairs which I had placed in the garden as imaginary opponents. My next move was to dart between the chairs, trap the ball, spin round quickly and kick the ball into an imaginary goal. At last I began to master the move, but my practice for that day ended suddenly when I connected with the ball before turning round, and sent it crashing through the kitchen window into the stew mother was preparing for dinner.

I was told my father would take the matter up with me when he came home from the shop, and I was so worried that I remained outside until hunger drove me in. I was not even reprimanded by my father, who probably realized I had had sufficient punishment with my childish fears—plus the hunger pains.

When I was eight, I was away from school with a poisoned toe. Greater than the pain of the toe was the agony of not being allowed to kick a ball. One afternoon my mother left me alone, while she went shopping. The temptation was too great for me. I borrowed a thickly padded tea-cosy, wrapped it round my injured foot, and hopped into the garden to practise ball-control.

I became so absorbed that time stood still. I heard my mother admonishing me. There were words from my father that evening, yet it was remarkable that my blood-poisoned toe began to heal with a speed that surprised the doctor, who does not know to this day the cause of the "cure." I am often reminded of the incident, because I still carry the scar on the big toe of my right foot.

CHAPTER II

SIGNED ON

I join Stoke at fifteen. . . . £1 a week for licking stamps. . . . Price of fitness. . . . A gold watch and goldfish. . . . I score eight goals as a centre-half. . . . Building castles. . . . Hair-raising fight stories. . . . Banking money.

WHEN I was fifteen Stoke City signed me as an amateur, and I received £1 a week to work in the office. My duties consisted of licking stamps, answering telephone calls and attending to any little jobs that Mr. Tom Mather, who was at this time manager of Stoke City might require.

Stoke had been watching me for a year, and the first approach made to my father when I was fourteen was promptly discouraged. Port Vale had also asked dad to give them an option on my services, and at this time I preferred the Hanley club, because I attended all their home games, hero-worshipping Bob Connelly, the centre-half, who carried the club on his shoulders for many years.

I was not allowed to develop a swollen head. My father saw to that. He seemed strict with me as a child, but as I grew older I realized how much I owed to him. From my earliest days he impressed on me the importance of fitness. He never drank or smoked in his life, and I have followed in his footsteps. To-day I take my training as seriously as when I was an up-and-coming player. I make a special point of concentrating on twenty yard sprints because I maintain a footballer who can outspeed the opposition over twenty yards has nothing to fear over 100 yards. It is the speed off the mark that is so important at football.

If I have given the impression that my search for fitness has always been a joy, I hasten to correct a false impression, because when I was only ten my father insisted I should join Jack, Arthur and himself in the morning exercises of deep breathing before an open window, followed by a spell with a chest expansioner. Regularly at six each morning I would wake as the sheets were pulled back off me. No matter how much I pleaded or what excuses I made, I had to join in what I used to term the "dawn torture." To-day I am forever grateful.

Dad was a great track fan, and was delighted when he discovered I was a useful runner at the age of six. He timed and trained me on Saturday mornings, and eventually entered me for the 100 yards in the Stoke-on-Trent sports which are still held each August. His purpose, no doubt, was to show me off to his friends.

I was terrified, and shed tears all the way to the ground. I was in such a state before the race was due to begin that dad pulled me out and I cried all the more realizing I had disgraced myself and dad.

I redeemed myself the following year when as a seven-year-old I was given 40 yards start in the 100 yards race and won my heats and the final—plus a gold watch. Dad was the proudest man in Stoke that afternoon, because although I had been given 40 yards I was competing against boys twice my age.

More than the gold watch, I treasured two goldfish my father gave me as a special prize, but both died after a few days, and there were more tears in the Matthews' home.

I entered the 100 yards in these annual sports until I was fourteen, and during that time won four first prizes and a second. The great day was when I won from scratch.

All the time I was running, my heart was really in football, I was still spending my spare time playing on the strip of waste land, and my greatest thrill came when I was chosen to represent Wellington Road School at the age of eleven. I usually played at centre-half, and one afternoon I scored 8 goals out of a 13 total from this position. For this feat I received sixpence from Mr. W. Terry, headmaster of the school. So it might be claimed I was the youngest ever professional footballer!

It was Mr. J. Slack, another master, who suggested I should try my hand at outside-right. I could not have shown up too badly in this position because the same year I was chosen to play for the North against the South in a schoolboys trial. Three weeks later I played for the English boys against the Rest at Kettering, and a few months later for England against Wales at Bournemouth.

Although I lived for football I had a boyish ambition to become a builder. Some young lads want to be engine-drivers or dust-men, but bricks and cement appealed to me and I am still fascinated by a builder mixing cement. It is one of my proud boasts that I could earn a living pointing a house.

But while I was dreaming of building my castles on weekdays, and playing football at the week-ends, Tom Mather had already approached my father about giving me a job in the offices of the Stoke Football Club. As always, my father was cautious, and told Mr. Mather, whom I never saw without a bowler hat, that I was too young to come to any definite decision.

Dad got as far as taking me to a builder he knew, and it was decided I should serve my apprenticeship in the art of bricks and mortar, but then dad made one of his sudden decisions, and my dreams of becoming a builder ended abruptly. "No, Stan," he said, "You come back home, and we'll spend another twelve months building you up. Health and fitness comes first, and this work will kill you."

So back I went to be built up. It was while hanging around the house doing little towards the family budget that the late Mr. Arthur Sherwin, then chairman of Stoke City, and Tom Mather made frequent "social" calls to see my father. Tom has a likeable personality, and was quite undaunted by the flat refusals he received whenever he broached the subject of my becoming a member of Stoke City's staff. Tom eventually succeeded in winning over my father, and I signed amateur forms.

Although I was now a member of Stoke City I continued to support Port Vale each Saturday. I remained in Mr. Mather's office for a year, and was then promoted to the dressing-room under the shrewd eye of Jimmy Vallance, Stoke's trainer, who was later to become my father-in-law. I was thrilled by my new experiences, and Mr. Vallance and Harry Pearson, the assistant trainer, took me under their wings, and I owe them both much for their kindness towards a gawky youth.

I was still fifteen when I played two games in the reserve side. A picture that will remain forever green in my memory, even should I live to be as old as Methuselah, is of my playing in my first match against Burnley reserves on the Stoke ground. We won 2—1, and my big thrill was to make the pass for Joe Mawson to score the first goal.

When I was sixteen I played in twenty-two games for our reserve team. I was, of course, still an amateur, and it was a generous gesture of the other Stoke players to give me two shillings each out of their £1 bonus whenever we won, which meant I had an extra £1 to take home on winning days.

Although Jack and Arthur were assistants in my father's shop, dad never tried to persuade me to become a hairdresser. It was a habit of mine, however, to go to the shop on Sunday mornings and give dad a hand as Jack and Arthur would take it in turns to have a morning off. My task was the simple one of lathering the faces of the customers in preparation for the more difficult job of shaving them. It meant a few extra coppers in tips, but I confess the reason I went was because I was fascinated listening to the exciting talk of fighting and football.

If dad could be drawn out of his modesty by an old friend he would tell stories of the old-time fighters that really made the hairs stand up on my young head. One day he was relating how an attempt had been made to bribe him, and how he had been threatened with violence unless he agreed to lose a certain fight. I had become so engrossed with the story of how he had managed to bluff the betting villains that I jabbed the soapy brush into the mouth of a customer who cursed me for my stupidity.

Sometimes I thought my father was hard with me, but to-day I am grateful for his thrift. While I was in the offices at Stoke he would not let me handle my own pocket money, and refused me money for my fares because he insisted the two miles from Hanley to Stoke four times a day would help in the building up that he said I required.

Fortunately, I had a wonderful ally in my mother, and some days she would slip me money for my bus fares. Dad had had to earn his money the hard way, and it was not unnatural that he should want me to appreciate it was easier to spend than earn.

Even when I signed professional forms at a salary of £5 a week in the football season and £3 weekly during the summer months he insisted I should take out a savings bank book, and my first deposit was the £10 received as a signing-on fee. Half my salary was deposited each week, and he saw to that I never missed a week.

Even the £1 bonus for a win in the reserve side had to be saved, but I was sometimes guilty of overlooking this rule, and would slip ten shillings in my pocket, and put the other ten shillings in my mother's hand with a wink. At first she protested saying there would be trouble if dad found out about it, but when she was hard-pressed she was glad of the few extra shillings. On the occasions she threatened to tell dad I chaffed her that she was now an accomplice to the " crime," and as such she dare not talk.

CHAPTER III

TOM MATHER'S VIGIL

A professional at seventeen. . . . Mr. Mather guards dad's shop. . . . I meet Betty. . . . Golfing with Sam English. . . . Married in Scotland

ON my seventeenth birthday I signed as a professional for Stoke City, and I think Tom Mather will bear me out that February 10, 1932 was one of the happiest days in his life. The weeks prior to my birthday had been hectic for the energetic Tom. He knew Port Vale were trying to persuade my father to take me over to Hanley, and what was even more dangerous to Tom's ambitions was the fact that Aston Villa had shown interest in me. Mr. Mather became a familiar figure in our house, and he visited my father's shop whenever he could find an excuse for a shave, haircut, massage or anything that would give him the opportunity to tell dad what great plans Stoke had for me.

Tom was really desperate, and confided that the signature meant so much that if Stoke lost me he would be in for the sack. Arthur Sherwin and Tom certainly went to great lengths to keep an eye on me two or three days before my birthday, and there was always somebody keeping watch to see if any other club managers or representatives visited my home or dad's shop. Mr. Sherwin himself took up guard in the pub opposite the shop where he had command of anyone approaching. Tom had scouts checking registration letters of cars arriving in Stoke with a special warning to beware of cars carrying Birmingham number plates.

Tom always has been an active manager, but on these few days he was like a man with St. Vitus's Dance until the morning of February 10, 1932, when my father said to me, "If you want to sign, Stan, it's all right with me." If St. Peter had smiled and said: "O.K. Tom, step through the Golden Gates, you've been promoted to Heaven," Tom Mather could not have shown more relief.

I played my first game in Stoke's League eleven soon afterwards at Bury, and it was a happy enough début because we won 1—0. It is funny how things stick in the memory, but I shall always recall this game because of the winning freak goal scored by Maloney, the Stoke left winger. Walter Bussy, the inside-right, centred on the eighteen-yards line, and Maloney cut into the centre. For some reason best known to himself the Bury goalkeeper came out to *head* the ball away, but Maloney nipped round him and scored. It is the only time I can recall a goalkeeper attempting to save a shot with his head.

I said it was a happy début for me because my team had won, but my form could not have been so hot because I did not play in the first eleven again that season. The following season, however, when I was eighteen I played in sixteen matches for our League side, and as Stoke City gained promotion to the First Division I qualified for a Second Division Championship medal.

I first met my wife when I was nineteen. Jimmy Vallance had been promising to teach me golf for many months, and one day during the off-season he called at the house, and asked if I would like to join him on a golfing holiday to Girvan in Ayrshire. I was thrilled at the chance. After Jimmy and I had been in Scotland a week, and I had lost more golf balls than I could afford, Betty Vallance joined us.

In those days Betty was a good golfer, and could naturally enough give me several strokes. I recall the day we met Sam English on the course. Sam was taking a practice swing with his driver when his caddy was not watching. It was a mighty swing, and caught the caddy unawares, completely knocking him out.

Sam made up a foursome, and as the "rabbit" of the party I was paired with Jimmy Vallance. It is to the credit of Jimmy that we won because I had "adopted" a slice that clung to me for the first nine holes, and more than one new ball was buried at sea.

Thanks to Jimmy and years of practice I now play off a ten handicap. Because Betty cannot beat me she reminds me of the days when she could give me strokes, and claims she taught me, anyway. Being a man of peace I will leave it at that.

I cannot pass on without a word about Sam English. Many readers will, of course, recall Sam was a great centre-forward with Glasgow Rangers. Unfortunately, he figured in one of Soccer's greatest tragedies when John Thomson, the Celtic goalkeeper, died as a result of an accident in which Sam was involved.

It happened during a League match between Rangers and Celtic at Ibrox Park, Glasgow, on September 5, 1931. Sam was through and had a chance to score when the fearless young Thomson dived at the Rangers' centre-forwards's feet, and sustained a fractured skull. Poor Thomson was carried off, and taken to hospital where he died the same evening. It was a tragic accident, and even more regrettable because the young Celtic goalkeeper had a wonderful career ahead of him, and would, I think, have joined Arsenal had he not met his death.

Poor Thomson! And poor Sam English! Sam was not to blame in any way, and was completely cleared by a Sheriff's jury verdict of accidental death, but he never really got over this tragedy. He later left Scotland to join Liverpool F.C. where he played some fine games, and scored many goals.

But back to Girvan. In that fortnight Betty and I saw much of each other, and our romance grew. A year later we became engaged. We were married in the club-house of the Bonnyton Golf Club near Glasgow. But it is more famous than as the place of our marriage, because—it will be recalled—Rudolph Hess landed on the course in 1941 after his fantastic flight from Germany. Hess landed at the fifth hole—probably the only time the Nazi ever holed out in one!

CHAPTER IV

CAPPED

A dream comes true. . . . The Carter partnership begins. . . . I swop jerseys with Roy John. . . . The roughest game of all. . . . Dropped for twelve months. . . . A German is too good for me.

I PLAYED my first game for England when I was nineteen, and being a kid I could hardly contain my excitement. There had been some rumours in Stoke that the English selectors might give "young Matthews" a chance against Wales at Cardiff on September 29, 1934.

I first heard the rumour that I had been chosen while in my father's shop. I did not waste a second, but dashed down the street to where the paper boy stood, and tossing half-a-crown snatched a paper that would either confirm my wildest dreams or else tell me the men in the barber's shop were pulling my leg.

It was there! Yes, indeed, a heading in large black type: "Matthews chosen for England." I shouted by delight, dashed my hand through the newsboy's mop of hair and told him to keep the change. I half walked and half ran back to my father. As proud as I was, dad was the proudest man in the world that day.

Call me vain if you like, but let my youth excuse me. I read the paper a dozen times, and such an impression did it make on my mind that I can rattle off the names of the England and Wales teams for that match without consulting my scrap book.

They were:

England: Hibbs (Birmingham), Cooper (Derby County), Hapgood (Arsenal), Britton (Everton), Barker (Derby County), Bray (Manchester City), Matthews (Stoke City), Bowden (Arsenal), Tilson (Manchester City), Westwood (Bolton Wanderers), Brook (Manchester City).

Wales: John (Preston North End), Lawrence (Swansea Town), Jones (Leicester City), Murphy (West Bromwich Albion), Griffiths (Middlesbrough), Richards (Wolverhampton Wanderers), Phillips (Wolverhampton Wanderers), O'Callaghan (Tottenham Hotspur), Williams (Newcastle United), Mills (Leicester City), Evans, W. (Tottenham Hotspur).

I can even remember the name of the referee, Mr. S. Thompson (Ireland). Yes, this was it, and it more than made up for my bitter disappointment at being omitted from the England team against Scotland at Hampden at the end of the previous season.

In the 1933–34 season I had been chosen for The Rest against England in the International trial at Sunderland. I was only eighteen, but had had a reasonably successful season. My partner in that trial was "Raich" Carter, then of Sunderland—and it was to be the first of many partnerships.

Even at this early stage in my career I knew Carter was an ideal partner, and at the end of the trial I felt satisfied I had done a good job of work, but the selectors must have thought otherwise. When the team to meet Scotland was announced Carter was inside-right, but Sammy Crooks was on the wing. Imagine my disappointment.

But back to the 1934–35 season. I had been given some recognition ten days before the international against Wales when the Football League chose me against the Irish League at Belfast. We won 6—1, and I scored a goal. That was the reason, of course, I had been hoping for ten days that my first "cap" would come.

I lived in a world of my own on the days preceeding the Cardiff game. I would lie awake for hours while my imagination ran riot. Some nights I was streaking down the wing at Ninian Park, beating four or five Welshmen, and finally cutting in to score the winning goal. I was mobbed by my colleagues, carried shoulder-high off the pitch, and given the reception of a hero on my return to Stoke. Thousands packed the streets while the Lord Mayor thanked me on behalf of Stoke and England.

Other nights I scored "hat-tricks" and some nights I dribbled the length of the field to bamboozle the Welsh defence. In my wanderings I was a sensation. How brave I was, lying comfortably in bed at night. I could face 40,000 Welshmen without turning a hair. But what a coward I was on the day of the match. Would I let England down? Would I be a disgrace to Stoke? I went as far as wishing I had not been picked at all. It was a question of stage fright.

In these moments of fear when we feel all alone a little act of friendliness or a word of encouragement means much, and I shall never forget Roy John's gesture. Roy was goalkeeper for Wales that day, and had not long joined Preston from Stoke City. He made a point of coming into the England dressing-room long before the game was due to start, and saw me sitting nervously in a corner of the room. I was already changed, although nobody else in the England team had started to get ready. Roy placed one of his large arms round my shoulder, and said kindly:

"Don't be scared, Stan. Like a dose of medicine, these internationals improve as they go on. You don't want to come off at the finish." John suggested we should exchange jerseys after the game. I readily agreed, not realizing I should later be scoring a goal against the man who was doing his best to help a kid to get over a state of nerves.

We took Wales comfortably that day. Freddie Tilson and Eric Brook, the Manchester City pair, were in great form. Tilson (2) and Brook scored. A minute after half-time I got my chance, and cutting in to take a Westwood pass I crashed the ball past my pal, Roy John.

I was too delighted to spare a thought for Roy. After all, hadn't I achieved the ambition of every footballer by scoring in my first international? Later I repented a little when Roy came in our dressing-room after the game, carrying his Welsh jersey over one arm:

"Here you are, Stan," he said without a trace of a smile. "Next time I open my big mouth, and waste sympathy on the likes of you—just shut me up, will you?" By now his eyes were twinkling, and I threw my English jersey to him. Roy is a great fellow, who will always have a warm corner in my heart.

The selectors were apparently satisfied with my showing against Wales. I was included in the Football League XI that beat the Scottish League 2—1 at Stamford Bridge the following October, and was picked for England again for that infamous match against Italy at Highbury on November 14, 1934.

But I have nothing to be pleased about over that game, the roughest in which I have ever taken part. It cost me my place in the England team. Geldard, Crooks, Worrall and Birkett were all put ahead of me on the list of outside-rights.

Fascism was flourishing in those days when England seemed oblivious of the danger and misery that was to smite the world only five years later. I am convinced the Italian masses did not want war, but Mussolini was trying to boost the morale of his countrymen, and if Italy could beat England at football in London it would be a triumph for Fascism. The bombastic Mussolini promised his footballers handsome bonuses if England were beaten.

What other promises of personal promotion were made I do not know, but the Italians certainly got " stuck in " to us right from the first whistle. They meant to win—at any price.

Eddie Hapgood was appointed captain for the first time because of an injury to the late Tom Cooper, the Derby County right-back, and England captain. The Arsenal skipper was not treated lightly by the Italians for before half-time he was carried to the dressing-room with a broken nose, the result of a blow from the elbow of one of Italy's forwards.

I have often wondered what was going on in the minds of Signor Grandi, the Italian Ambassador, and the late Prince Arthur of Connaught who sat together in the Highbury stand. The English players were disgusted, and so were 50,000 spectators who had come to Highbury to see a game of football, and instead had witnessed a brawl.

The match blew up after England made a flying start. In the first minute we were awarded a penalty. Eric Brook, usually a deadly shot, took the kick, which looked a certain winner to me, but I had not bargained for the agility of Ceresoli, the Italian goalkeeper, who made the daring young man on the flying trapeze look like an old man with rheumatism with the ease with which he dived across the goal to stop Eric's pile-driver.

Ten minutes later Brook more than made up for this miss, heading in my spinning centre after I had run round Allemandi, Italy's left-back. The tough little Brook had a head of iron, and Ceresoli never saw the ball shoot off the Manchester City winger's blond head.

Neither did Italy's goalkeeper know what was happening soon afterwards when yet another free kick was awarded to England, when one of our players had his feet kicked from under him some yards outside the penalty area. Brook took the kick. This time he left Ceresoli dumb-founded, and he did not have a chance against the best free kick I have ever seen.

The Italians went crazy. It was then that Hapgood's nose was broken. Monti, Italy's captain and centre-half, left with an injury to his foot. Our boys were rattled.

It was fortunate for England that Brook and Wilf Copping, the Arsenal left-half, now trainer to Southend United F.C., were playing. Eric and Wilf enjoyed themselves that day as never before, after they themselves had been handled roughly. Brook, his shoulder strapped, and Copping, with many bruises, gave the Eye-ties something to think about—not by foul tactics, but by real honest-to-goodness English shoulder-charging. They did their duty that day for England, and if ever it could be said two men won a match, it was Copping and Brook on this infamous occasion.

After Monti left with a splintered bone in his foot, there was hardly any holding Italy.

Ted Drake, who came in as a late substitute for Fred Tilson at centre-forward, was being "blooded" in his first international. He had the satisfaction of scoring to give England a 3—0 lead, but young Ted had to be carried off later.

We were on the run in the second half. When Meazza, Italy's centre-forward, cracked in two goals in quick succession it looked as though Italy would at least save the game, or perhaps win it.

It was then Brook, Copping, Frank Moss in goal, Hapgood; and Male worked like heroes, and when at last I heard the final whistle, I sighed with relief. It had been a bad match for me.

I dare not leave this match without satisfying the curiosity of many readers as to the number of Arsenal players in the England team that day. There were seven, and this was a club record for an international match.

Five Arsenal men were originally chosen, but when Cooper and Tilson dropped out, George Male and Ted Drake came in.

The two teams were:

England: Moss (Arsenal), Male (Arsenal), Hapgood (Arsenal), Britton (Everton), Barker (Derby County), Copping (Arsenal), Matthews (Stoke City), Bowden (Arsenal), Drake (Arsenal), Bastin (Arsenal), Brook (Manchester City).

Italy: Ceresoli (Ambrosiana), Monzeglio (Bologna), Allemandi (Ambrosiana), Ferraris (Lazio), Monti (Juventus), Bertolini (Juventus), Guaita (Rome), Serantoni (Ambrosiana), Meazza (Ambrosiana), Ferrari (Juventus), Orsi (Juventus).

The selectors dropped me for twelve months after this game. I might not have got back for years, but for a lucky break for me, and an unlucky one for Ralph Birkett, the Middlesbrough right-winger who had been transferred from Arsenal. Ralph had been chosen as England's outside-right for the visit of Germany at Tottenham on December 4, 1935.

Incidentally, the Germans were one of the first international football teams to travel by air. The Moscow Dynamos flew here ten years later, and R.A.F. and Army teams flew during the war. The match against Germany was fixed for a Wednesday. Birkett had the misfortune to be injured in a League match on the Saturday, and so the selectors called on me.

Often a footballer playing at the top of his form loses his international place for keeps through an injury. A substitute is brought in who impresses the selectors, with the result that the original choice does not get back. But this was not to be the case here. England beat Germany easily enough by three goals to nil, but I did not have a good match, and Birkett was selected for the next international.

My father and two brothers had been anxious to see me make good, and borrowed an old car to drive to London from Hanley, and it must have been a disappointed party on the homeward journey.

There were two good reasons why I failed. The first was Muenzenberg, Germany's left-back, who was too quick and too experienced for me. The second, that I made the worst miss of my career quite early in the game, when I had the ball at my toe several yards inside the penalty area. I was certain I would score. I took a great kick, but kicked the turf. The ball did not travel more than five yards. It was the first time I really heard a 40,000 crowd groan like one gigantic voice. This miss destroyed my confidence, and the player who loses his confidence might as well return to the dressing-room. Muenzenberg was at the peak of his form that day at Tottenham. His positioning was superb. He tackled easily, and was yards faster. The only consolation came three years later when we thrashed the Nazis in Berlin. Three years on a football field is a long time. I had gained in experience, my confidence was greater, and Muenzenberg had slowed up considerably. But more about that Berlin triumph later.

CHAPTER V

THE FIGHTING BARBER

His wax moustache. . . . When the time-keeper forgot to check his watch. . . . A trip to Manchester. . . . Footwork. . . . Detained at the police station.

I MAKE no apologies for devoting a chapter to my father. I wish he were alive to read these few words dedicated to his memory. In the last few years of his life he was a tired-looking little man with a small moustache and thinning grey hair, who worked long hours in his shop.

It would be a little difficult, therefore, to picture him as a sprightly young man with a wax moustache, who took part in boxing contests all over the country—for the sheer love of fighting.

He owned a barber's shop as a young man, and was naturally enough named the " Fighting Barber " by the boxing writers of his day. Some of the old-timers wrote that if he had taken the game up earlier he would probably have won a British championship.

As it was he was one of the best fighters turned out by North Staffordshire, and his record included 350 fights of which he lost only nine.

He was one of the few boxers to have fought in the ring with a waxed moustache. Even the great John L. Sullivan, former heavy-weight champion of the world, shaved his moustache off before a contest.

He shaved and cut his customers' hair by day, and trained in an old gymnasium in Etruria Road, Hanley, by night. He had exceptional speed, astonishing footwork, and soon became famous throughout the halls of North Staffordshire in the days when fighters had to be really outstanding to get by.

His name and fame spread, and he became a favourite at the most exclusive sporting club in the country, the old National Sporting Club, the premises of which to-day are used as a banana warehouse.

On of my father's greatest victories was over Tancy Lee, the remarkable Scot, who won a Lonsdale Championship belt and who scored a sensation earlier by beating Jimmy Wilde.

One of his last fights was against Tommy Harrison, the Hanley featherweight, who died some years ago. The fight went the full twenty rounds, and ended in a draw after a struggle that caused so much interest that I still hear old-timers in Hanley recall incidents from it. Curiously, dad and Tommy Harrison had also fought during the first great war when they were serving in the North Staffords. On that occasion dad received the decision.

Perhaps his greatest fight was on May 18, 1912, when he met George Mackness, of Kettering, at the National Sporting Club. It was his debut at the club, and the well-to-do members who sat at the ringside in evening dress with diamond cuffs and studs and glittering rings had not even heard of Jack Matthews or George Mackness.

But the fight that followed was one that none who saw it will ever forget. Even the timekeeper forgot to check his stop-watch, with the result that one round lasted five minutes instead of three! I am writing what follows from an old clipping in my scrap-book.

" The contest was scheduled for ten rounds, but both boxers began as though in a hurry to get to their respective homes. Jack Matthews began standing upright and pushing a straight left into the face of Mackness, but on being punched on the nose tore into Mackness with both hands, dropping him for a count of four with a neat right cross to the jaw. Both boxers fought toe-to-toe for almost a minute before Mackness was down for another short count. The Kettering boxer was up in a shot and fought back with such fury that before the first round ended Matthews was on the floor.

" After that hectic first three minutes the Corinthians at the ringside might well have expected a quieter second round, but not so. In the second round the Hanley featherweight connected with a left hook, and Mackness dropped. 'He just can't get up,' a ringsider shouted, but he struggled to both feet, leaping at his opponent with a right swing that knocked him clean off his feet.

"It was a great punch, and Matthews only just managed to beat the count. He fought back, and kept on both feet for nearly half a minute, but Mackness was now on top, and another right-swing put the Fighting Barber down for eight.

"Matthews kept fighting back, but was once again sent down—very nearly for the full count. The Kettering fighter was delivering his blows with much accuracy and power, and had the measure of his opponent. Yet in spite of this and the fact that he had been on the canvas three times in this round Matthews actually began forcing the fight.

"As they stood toe-to-toe like a couple of fighting cocks some club members stood up and shouted in their excitement.

Mackness was dropped for eight, but being as tough as they make them, the Kettering boxer fought back to drop the Hanley man for three successive counts. Such was the excitement that the time-keeper forgot to call 'Time' until a ringsider shouted: 'Man, what's the time, for heaven's sake.' It was discovered the round had lasted five minutes in which Matthews paid eight visits to the floor, while Mackness was knocked over four times.

"It was anybody's fight as both boxers went to their corners, although Mackness had been made a slight favourite. The third round was another hectic session, but it is a credit to the skill and fairness of both fighters that amid all their fury, not one blow was landed that brought even a warning from the referee.

"The Fighting Barber paid three visits to the canvas in this round, and Mackness was down twice. Ringsiders were astonished in the fourth round when, in spite of the heavy punishment they had sustained, both boxers appeared to be as fresh as ever, although if either appeared the worse for wear it was Jack Matthews.

"It came as a shock, therefore, when Matthews met Mackness in the centre of the ring, and after exchanging a dozen or more blows connected with a right and a left to the Kettering fighter's head, and sent Mackness down and out for the full count."

This climax was too much for the onlookers, who, according to the writer at the National Sporting Club, waved their fists, and shouted "Bravo!" There was not any quietening them as Mackness's seconds dragged their unconscious man to his corner, and forced his head into a bucket of cold water.

My father always maintained that this was his greatest fight, but simple man that he was, he got more enjoyment at winning a bout at Manchester, when he was little more than a novice. He had not opened his shop in Hanley for many months when he was approached by Mr. Jack McNiff, a well-known promoter.

Mr. McNiff had been watching a local boy by the name of Chambers, who boasted of more than twenty knockouts, at the City Athletic Club in Manchester. A Manchester inn-keeper offered anybody a wager they could not find a novice capable of beating Chambers. Jack McNiff accepted the challenge, and set about finding a boxer good enough to beat Chambers. It was while on the look-out in the gymnasium in Etruria Road, that he saw dad sparring, and was so impressed that he offered him the fight in Manchester.

My father was delighted at getting a chance of going to Manchester, but when McNiff visited the City Athletic Club and told them he was bringing a young barber from Hanley to fight Chambers, the match-maker of the club declared that as he had never heard of Jack Matthews, he would not pay him to fight such a clever boxer as Chambers.

So Mr. McNiff promised that if Matthews did not put up a good show he would pay the Hanley lad's purse money and expenses. The match-maker, having nothing to lose, agreed to stage the fight. My father shaved his customers all day, and when the last client had been dealt with, he hurried to the gym to train with his brother Charlie.

Charlie was useful with his fists, and made an ideal sparring partner. On the night of the fight, my father, Uncle Charlie and Mr. McNiff arrived outside the City Athletic Club in Manchester, and met another Potteries fighter, Tim Coleman, who had walked from Oldham to see dad box. Coleman volunteered to act as a second. The match-maker was not impressed by the skinny appearance of the Hanley barber, and expressed his hope that the fight would last a few rounds to give his customers good value.

Chambers began the fight with such confidence that he obviously thought dad was another "push-over," but so good was my father's footwork that Chambers began missing by inches, and sometimes feet. This made him angry, but the more angry he became the more he was made to miss, and in the third and fourth rounds Jack Matthews was scoring freely with well-placed straight lefts.

When the fifth round started the Manchester boy had completely lost his confidence and his head. He swung madly, and all dad had to do was step aside and score with a left. Midway through the round he stepped aside, and as Chambers rushed madly forwards connected with a right to the chin which sent the Manchester boy down for the full count.

Some Manchester sportsmen were so pleased with the performance by Jack Matthews that they offered to set him up in a hairdressing saloon in the city. But dad loved the Potteries, and could never be persuaded to leave Hanley. If he had changed his mind I suppose I should never have played football for Stoke City.

Obviously, I never saw my father's footwork when he was young, but I am told it was really remarkable. It has been submitted that I inherited his dancing feet, but used them for football instead of boxing. Whether that is so I do not know, but if it is true it is just another asset I owe to a wonderful man.

Before I close this chapter on Jack Matthews I must tell you how once he was scared out of his life, and almost gave up his career as a boxer.

He was boxing at Liverpool Stadium against an opponent whose name I cannot recall at the time of writing. Dad hit him so hard in the fifth round that he remained unconscious for some hours, with the result that my father was detained at a Liverpool police station all night. If the boxer had died dad would have been charged with manslaughter, and he felt pretty sick. Fortunately the fighter recovered, and dad was released, but it was the nearest shave the "Fighting Barber" ever had.

CHAPTER VI

TROUBLE AT STOKE

I ask for a transfer, and am refused. . . . Stoke ask me to play in the reserves, and I refuse. . . . I meet the directors behind locked doors. . . . Loyal friends. . . .

IN my seventeen years with Stoke City I enjoyed some of the happiest hours any man could wish for, and considering I have been with only two clubs since I was fifteen I have had very few ups and downs. I defy any footballer—international or third team player—to boast he has never been dissatisfied or disgruntled at some period in his career. It does not only apply to footballers, because it is only human at times to experience frustration and to feel unappreciated.

Of course, I am truly happy at Blackpool, but the big slice of my career was carved in the Potteries, and I should like to say for the benefit of loyal Stoke fans that only three times in seventeen years was I unhappy with the City.

The first uproar was early in 1938 when I asked Stoke City to place my name on the transfer list, and again when I refused to play in the reserve side on October 19, 1946, after reporting fit following a leg injury that not only kept me out of the Stoke eleven for several weeks, but also lost me two " caps " against Ireland in Belfast and Eire in Dublin at the end of September.

The third occasion was in April 1947, when Bob McGrory, the manager, and I had words. It was not because I was dropped that annoyed me so much as the fact that the Stoke manager would not give me a definite answer as to how I stood. It was after this incident that the directors agreed to transfer me to Blackpool at the end of the 1946–47 season.

Each incident was reported as sensational, and when I refused to play with the " Stiffs "—as football supporters speak of reserve sides—I was more in the news than Hermann Goering, who the same week had cheated the Allied hangman by taking his own life, swallowing a phial of cyanide of potassium a few hours before the time fixed for his execution. The telephone in my hotel was going night and day, and eventually I was forced to stay away from the hotel, eating meals out to avoid phone calls and photographers.

I think it was a series of misunderstandings that made a mountain of trouble out of what was really a mole-hill. Perhaps both sides mishandled the affair a little, and overnight it had grown into a crisis.

Let me tell the true facts which I hope will give both sides of the story. Early in September when Stoke City were playing Manchester United, I ran for the ball and suddenly felt a twitch of pain in my right leg. I had pulled a thigh muscle, and finished the game more or less a passenger.

Obviously, I was out of the Stoke team for some weeks, but I was anxious to get fit for the internationals in Belfast and Dublin at the end of the month, and I was confident that I would be recovered in good time. I was chosen by the English selectors, but to my great disappointment, had to cry off a few days before the party sailed for Belfast. The leg was not quick to mend, and I did not want to take any chances, so I did not rush to return to the Stoke City side. In the meantime, Stoke were doing extremely well, and had gone six weeks without losing. On October 12, Stoke went to Chelsea, and before 68,000 fans trounced the London club 5—2. The Press were full of praise for Stoke, and for George Mountford, who was deputising for me on the right wing. Stoke's match on the following Saturday was against Arsenal at Highbury, and now quite fit, I was particularly anxious to make my come-back in London, and against Arsenal of all clubs. Bob McGrory was not so anxious. He suggested it might be as well for me to have a run with the reserves. I emphasize here that the Stoke manager did not order me to play in the second team, but only suggested it, so that contrary to some stories at the time when I declined the suggestion I was not defying either the Stoke manager or the directors.

I was in a perilous position. Football is my livelihood, and once I begin slipping I intend getting out of the game, but I had no reason to believe that I had already started to slip. If I agreed to play with the reserves, and Stoke's first team continued their successful run, I might have remained in the reserves for weeks, months or all the season. I hope I shall not be accused of being swollen-headed, but I do consider myself worthy of a place in League football.

[*Daily Express*

Front page news over a period of ten years.

The newspapers seized upon the differences between myself and my club. Every paper carried a front page story next day, and what hurt me most of all was a report that the Stoke players had sent a deputation to the management requesting I should not return in place of George Mountford.

From this moment onwards I was given little peace. The news-hounds were chasing me for statements, and the postman began delivering poison-pen letters, some of which accused me of poor sportsmanship. However, the post brought one letter that made up for all the cheap stuff from anonymous writers. It was from Neil Franklin, the Stoke and England centre-half, denying there was any truth in the reports that the players were against me. Neil had resented the suggestion, and had called together the whole team, asking anybody who had approached the management to own up. Nobody stepped forward, and Neil asked if he could deny the statement on behalf of the team. They all nodded agreement. This was reassuring news because obviously if it had been true that the rest of the team did not like me I could not have remained with Stoke, and would have had no other alternative than to ask to be placed on the transfer list.

Never at any time during this difference did I make the request to be put on the transfer list, although stories were being circulated that I was going to join Blackpool. Other stories reported Chelsea, Arsenal, Newcastle and Aston Villa seeking my transfer. They were not true. Headlines stated if I should be transferred £20,000 would go into the till at Stoke but I never considered myself to be a £20,000 footballer. In fact, Blackpool eventually handed Stoke City a cheque for £11,500 for my services on May 10, 1947, but I had cut out any competitive bids by stating that I would only go to Blackpool.

While the rumours grew, and the phone bell rang incessantly I continued to go about my normal business. I attended to correspondence concerning the hotel, and trained on the Blackpool ground each morning. I never spared myself, and knew I was fitter than when I had played for Stoke against Manchester United in the F.A. Cup the previous season. On that occasion the Stoke directors had chosen me without suggesting I should have a fitness test in the reserves.

Stoke went to Arsenal, and I stayed in Blackpool. Stoke were strong favourites to beat Arsenal, who so far that season had not won a match at Highbury, but they did not have a good day, and the London team claimed their first home win with a 1—0 victory. George Mountford did not play up to his usual standard. I was sorry for him. I had no quarrel with him, because he is a grand fellow, and a good footballer. It was unfortunate he should also become a victim of publicity.

Bob McGrory later contacted me in Blackpool, and I agreed to go to Stoke the following Tuesday to meet the directors. Reports were printed that Alderman Harry Booth, our 70-year-old chairman, was going to reprimand me, and insist I must train at Stoke.

I had announced earlier that I intended taking a rest from the game for two more Saturdays, and Jock Dodds suggested I should go over to Dublin with him for a few days. Jock, of course, had caused a stir himself a few months earlier when he had refused to sign on for Blackpool, and chose to sign a contract to play for the Irish club, Shamrock Rovers. Mrs. Joe Cunningham, the only woman director in football, did the signing on, and Jock had £20 a match terms, which is quite different to payment in the English League.

I motored to Stoke on the Tuesday, and met my directors behind locked doors. It was a friendly meeting, and both sides pointed out grievances, and agreed that perhaps the business had been handled a little hastily. We finished with handshakes all round after a two-hour discussion. The directors agreed to my request for a week's rest, and also agreed I should be allowed to continue to train at Blackpool, because it would be impossible for me to look after the hotel if I spent most of my time in Stoke. There was never any ultimatum from either side.

Reporters and photographers were admitted afterwards, and photos were taken of myself shaking the directors by the hand, and an official bulletin issued to the reporters read:

"The differences between the board and Stanley Matthews have been amicably settled, but owing to the publicity of the last few days Matthews has asked the board to grant him a week's holiday. This had been agreed. The verdict was unanimous." And so the whole unfortunate incident that had lasted a week ended, and was I glad?

The other difference with the club in 1938 seems a long, long time ago, but it caused chaos at Stoke. Perhaps it was because I was eight years younger, but whatever it was I know I was staggered by the limelight afforded to the one and only occasion I requested to be placed on the transfer list.

It happened that I was browned-off, and wanted a change of club and atmosphere, so I approached the directors, believing my request would be accepted without much ado, but this was not so. Mr. Booth and his board invited me to meet them to discuss the reasons for my request. I explained I was not happy at Stoke, but hastened to assure the board that the reason for my intended departure was not due to any of my colleagues in the Stoke team, in spite of the rumour in the city that bad feeling had developed between myself and one or two of the players. This was quite untrue.

After an hour's discussion the board declined to accept my request until I had thought the matter over again. I was asked to reconsider my decision. Next day, I decided to get away from Stoke because I could not make a move in the street without being stopped, and dragged into arguments that did not always concern me. I asked for leave of absence, which the directors granted me. I chose to visit Blackpool, for the first time in my life—not realising I would be stationed there during the war, and that it was to become my permanent home.

The seven days following my request to be transferred were as hectic as the seven days following my refusal to play in the reserves. Football reporters from London phoned day and night. Some of them made special journeys from London to interview me, and although some of my best friends are journalists, I was so sick of the whole business that often I had to give them the slip to get a little peace and relaxation. It was soon rumoured that Everton, Bolton Wanderers, Derby County, Leicester City and Manchester City were interested in obtaining my signature. Everton, Leicester and Aston Villa had already approached Stoke for my signature, before I had made my request to leave the club.

Newcastle United, who had offered £10,000 for me in 1935, were soon on the trail, and my old friend Tom Mather, at this time managing Newcastle, travelled overnight with a blank cheque in his pocket. He was accompanied by Mr. A. G. Stableforth, a director, who was prepared to pay whatever price Stoke might place on my head.

Amid all this commotion, I had one great consolation, and that was the wonderful support given me by the people of Stoke and Hanley. I knew I had many friends in the city and town, but I had never realized how really staunch they were. Within a few hours of the headlines in the " Evening Sentinel " declaring that I was not happy at Stoke, seven leading industrialists got together and decided to call a public protest meeting in the King's Hall the following Monday.

Soon every hoarding seemed to bear one of the familiar " Stanley Matthews Must Not Go ! " bills that the industrialists had had printed. Advertisements were put into the local Press, and, of course, there were many editorial comments. The actual wording of the handbills advertising the meeting which was convened by Messrs. R. Lewis Johnson, Ashley Myott, E. H. Bailey, A. B. Jones (Jun.) Arthur Gaunt, T. B. Roberts and Sidney H. Dodd, was:

STANLEY MATTHEWS MUST NOT GO!

PUBLIC MEETING OF STOKE CITY SUPPORTERS

King's Hall, Stoke
Monday Next, 7.30 p.m.

TO URGE THE RETENTION OF STANLEY MATTHEWS

The poster that stopped a city working.

Three thousand Stoke City fans attended, and more than a thousand, who could not get inside the hall, paraded the streets demanding I should not leave Stoke. It was claimed by some of the industrialists that the controversy was undermining output in the Potteries. To me it all seemed a little crazy that by asking to be placed on the transfer list I should be disrupting the workings of a city!

It was decided at this meeting, presided over by Mr. Ashley Myott, chairman of the Wages and Conditions Committee of the British Manufacturers Federation, that a deputation should meet the Stoke directors and myself at separate meetings. In the meantime I had again met Mr. Booth, Stoke City Chairman, at his own request but had refused to change my decision.

On February 15, 1938—a week after my request—the directors announced they had declined to accept my request, which meant I would have to remain with the club until the first week in May, when the 1938-39 season ended. I could have appealed to the Football League for intervention, but that was not necessary.

Fortunately for me, the voices of the supporters had not been raised in vain, and after the deputation from the Protest Meeting had visited the directors and myself, difficulties began to be smoothed out, and I was given an assurance that efforts would be made to make me more comfortable in the future.

I stayed to enjoy a further nine happy years, and whatever those grand football fans of the Potteries think of me to-day, I can say in all sincerity that I always did my best to entertain them, and to pull my weight for Stoke City. Now I shall endeavour to serve Blackpool with the same loyalty. Already I have found a warmth from these Lancashire fans that I sensed in the Potteries. Footballers are only human, and need encouragement and sympathy at some time. I have found both at Stoke and Blackpool.

I have played football in many parts of the world. More than once I have been surprised to hear the North Staffs dialect floating from the terraces packed with German, Italian or Portugese crowds and declaring: "Play up Stoke City" or "Good old Blackpool." It is encouraging to hear English words of encouragement in a strange land.

Stoke fans stuck by me in foul weather as well as when the sun shone, and it was more than I deserved when the football supporters of the city started a public testimonial for me after I had broken Eddie Hapgood's record of appearances for England. When I played against Belgium at Wembley on January 19, 1946 it was my forty-fourth appearance—one more than Eddie's previous record. And now at Blackpool I am still among friends.

I am grateful also to the Football Association and appreciated the address and the certificates presented to me when I broke the international appearances record. Football has been kind to me. But most important of it all it has provided me with thousands of true friends. They are on the terraces each week.

CHAPTER VII

STRANGE CASE OF FREDDIE STEELE

Loss of form. . . . Darkened rooms and strange dreams. . . . Scoring with a loose cartilage! . . . Freddie, successful manager, and still playing well, joins Port Vale. . . . Three Stoke players chosen for England. . . . Beaten by the Hampden Roar. . . . We end the Hampden bogy.

HAVE you ever heard of psychiatry in football? I suppose you would ridicule a fiction writer who chose a plot in which his hero was a professional footballer who had lost his nerve, but as a result of treatment from a psychiatrist went on the field and scored freely? I would have joined in the scoffing until I saw this very thing happen to Freddie Steele, Stoke City's centre-forward.

In 1938-39 season Freddie's spirits had sunk pretty low. His old knee injury was troubling him, he was worried about his wife who was at that time expecting a baby. Altogether his world seemed black.

In the first half of the season he scored only nine goals, and Stoke were in a dangerously low position in the League. He was rested from the team, and while doctors could not decide whether to recommend an operation for the removal of a cartilage it was the opinion of many of his friends at Stoke that the root of the trouble would be found in Freddie's mind rather than his knee.

He had developed an inferiority complex, and was so depressed that once or twice he openly confessed he doubted if he would ever play football again. Weeks went by, and eventually Bob McGrory suggested, as a last resort, that Freddie should consult a well-known nerve specialist in the Potteries. Steele was so desperate that he agreed to try anything rather than sit around brooding. Freddie visited the psychiatrist twice a day for several weeks.

The treatment was carried out in the doctor's study. The room was darkened, Freddie sat on one side of the fire-place while the specialist, who always wore a dark suit, sat on the other side. All that Steele could see were two piercing eyes staring at him, and occasionally he would catch a glimpse of the clear-cut features of the doctor in the flickering fire-light.

The specialist insisted Steele should talk about his childhood, his domestic life, and his dreams. Special attention was given to dreams, and Freddie slept with a pencil and note-book beside his bed so that he could jot down incidents no matter how trivial or crazy, immediately he awoke.

Day after day the voice behind those two piercing eyes assured him he was a great footballer. That he could go out and score goals if he so desired. The treatment showed promise of success because it was noticed by Bob McGrory and the players that Eddie was far happier than before. He arrived at the ground some mornings whistling, and was certainly more confident. He once admitted the nets were looking larger than ever before.

Stoke decided to give him a run with the first team against Huddersfield, and on the Friday he went off to his specialist. After a long session the doctor implored him not to let him down to-morrow. Freddie didn't either. He went out and scored, and furthermore went on to score ten goals in five League matches. What is even more remarkable is the fact that all the time Steele was playing with a loose cartilage ! He later underwent an operation. The success of any treatment that can make a player with cartilage trouble go out and score goals is beyond all doubt. I certainly would not believe it to have been possible had I not seen it for myself.

Freddie has had a longer run in the game than most players. He left Stoke to become a successful player-manager with Mansfield. The Third Division Northern Section club had a good Cup and League run with Steele guiding them as manager and scoring goals, and there were sad hearts at Mansfield when, with not many days of 1951 remaining, Freddie took on the job as player-manager of Port Vale. Apart from the fact that it was a more attractive offer, the real deciding factor was that in taking over at Port Vale, Freddie was returning home because he was born close to the Vale's ground at Hanley.

While the Mansfield directors sportingly stood aside for Freddie to make his own choice, the officials and members of the Mansfield Supporters Club made an appeal for Steele to remain with them. Freddie would have been happy to oblige, but all of us knew in our hearts that there is no place like home.

Steele is one of the cleverest centre-forwards I have seen. Of course, I never saw Hughie Gallacher or Dixie Dean at their best.

He is not a big fellow as centre-forwards go, for while he stands only 5 ft 9 ins. he is not heavily built. But such are his skill and shooting powers that he is for ever dangerous to the best defence in the country. Furthermore, he is not the type of centre-forward who relies on spoon-feeding from his inside-forwards Steele is a first-rate ball distributor, and can hold his line together with exceptional skill. Perhaps the reason for this is that he began his career as an inside-right, and never lost his science when he became a centre-forward.

Freddie was working as a potter when Stoke discovered him. He was only eighteen at the time, but his rise to fame was rocket-like. He began scoring regularly for Stoke's League side. He was chosen to lead the Football League against the Irish League at Belfast and the greatest honour in the game came his way soon afterwards when he was picked for England in 1937.

He had successful matches against Wales at Cardiff and Ireland at Stoke. A leg injury kept him out of the England XI against The Rest in the international trial at Burnley on March 17, but in spite of this the England selectors chose him for the gruelling test against Scotland at Hampden Park the following April.

This was a great day for Stoke because Joe Johnson was selected as the outside-left, and I was chosen for the right wing—the first time in the history of Stoke that three of its players had been chosen for England against Scotland, although Rowley, Clare and Underwood, former Stoke players, had once provided the England defence against Ireland.

There is only one sad twist to this Stoke record, and that is that England were beaten 3—1 before 149,407—the biggest crowd for any football match with possible exception of the first Cup Final at Wembley between Bolton Wanderers and West Ham in 1923 when the crowd broke in, and anything between 150,000 and 200,000 saw the game.

England led Scotland 1—0 at half-time as the result of a goal by Steele five minutes before the interval, after Ronnie Starling and and Joe Johnson had tricked Scotland's defence.

The England team played exceptionally well in this half. Everything had worked to the plan discussed at our hotel after breakfast. We had been told to swing the ball from wing to wing, and to make a gap down the middle for Steele.

Cliff Britton of Everton and Jack Bray of Manchester City, were the key men behind England's attack while Alf Young, the Huddersfield Town " stopper," was to break up the attempts of Walker and McPhail to put Frank O'Donnell through. I was opposing Andrew Beattie for the first time. This was Beattie's début in a Hampden game, and although in the years that followed Andy and I have had some exciting duels the luck was in my favour on this occasion, and Beattie could do little more than chase my shadow.

With Johnson and Starling sending across sweeping passes to "Raich" Carter and myself, the Scottish defence was for ever caught on the wrong foot, and we were indeed a happy set of boys when we left the field at half-time five minutes after Steele had given England the lead.

George Male, the England captain, and Alf Young, were light-hearted during the interval. Alf was delighted at the way things were working out. Perhaps we were over-confident. Perhaps we had under-estimated the fighting spirit of Scotland. Perhaps we had not bargained for the intensity of the Hampden Roar. I had, of course, heard about this war-cry of the Scottish football fan, but had never previously experienced it. Those of you who have never heard the "Roar" cannot appreciate the effect it has on a player. It shook me and my colleagues in the England team.

If ever a match was won and lost by a roar it was this game. You could sense the enthusiasm of the crowd being transfused into the veins of the Scottish players. Two minutes after the interval Frank O'Donnell equalized. The credit for this goal must go to Tommy Walker, who seized on a pass from the wing, zig-zagged his way goalwards, and found O'Donnell with one of those delightful through-passes that are Walker's own speciality. As the match progressed so did the roar become more terrible—for us. It shook our confidence and left our legs a little uncertain. As the roar grew in volume so did Scotland seem to get a stronger grip on the game. I knew within myself we could not now win. Our nerves had cracked, and when Bob McPhail beat Vic Woodley from fifteen yards out with only twelve minutes remaining the game was as good as over.

To make Scotland's win even more convincing McPhail headed a third goal three minutes from the end, and so we lost 3—1 after having outplayed the Scots in the first half. Even Scottish journalists considered England to be a little unlucky, and some declared it was the best England eleven seen at Hampden in years.

The teams that day were:

Scotland: Dawson (Rangers), Anderson (Hearts), Beattie (Preston N.E.), Massie (Aston Villa), Simpson (Rangers), Brown (Rangers), Delaney (Celtic), Walker (Hearts), O'Donnell, F. (Preston N.E.), McPhail (Rangers), Duncan (Derby County).

England: Woodley (Chelsea), Male (Arsenal), Barkas (Manchester City), Britton (Everton), Young (Huddersfield Town), Bray (Manchester City), Matthews (Stoke City), Carter (Sunderland), Steele (Stoke City), Starling (Aston Villa), Johnson (Stoke City).

The only consolation to that defeat came two years later when we laid the Hampden bogy, beating Scotland 2—1 with a goal by Lawton from my pass ninety seconds from time. It was our first win at Hampden since 1927, and was to be the last official international match between England and Scotland for eight years owing to war.

This time it was England who were a goal down with only twenty minutes to go. The " Roar " was as great as ever, the bagpipes screamed loudly and it rained as it had never rained before. But this time we were well on top, and nothing could undermine our confidence or dampen our spirits. Nevertheless, things had not gone too well at the start. Apart from the handicap of playing against a strong wind that blew the rain into our faces, sometimes blinding our vision, Jimmy Dougal, the Preston centre-forward, put Scotland in front after twenty minutes. It was a " gift " goal, and many thought we would not fight back as strongly as we did in the second half. The goal had come about when the defence passed back to the goalkeeper, and the ball slowed up in the mud, and Dougal, who did not appear in a scoring position, nipped in before Woodley was able to get to the ball.

The wind abated in the second half, and the downpour became little more than a gentle shower. England went on the attack, but although we were undeniably on top of the Scots, and only the mudlarking of that wonderful goalkeeper Jerry Dawson of Glasgow Rangers kept us out, it was twenty minutes before we equalized, when Pat Beasley, the Huddersfield Town left-winger cracked the ball past Dawson with his left foot.

This goal restored our confidence, and the Scots became a little shaky, but it was not until ninety minutes from the final whistle that we definitely smashed the Hampden bogy. I recall the winning move as though it were yesterday. The referee was glancing at his watch, and the game looked a certain draw. Then Len Goulden, England's inside-left, darted across the field and slipped the ball to me. I cut inside and down the wing. I could see the sturdy form of Tommy Lawton rushing goalwards, so I centred. It worked perfectly.

Up went Tommy, and that shining black head nodded the ball into the net. The England team could hardly contain its excitement as we shook hands like a bunch of school-kids. Eddie Hapgood, normally undemonstrative, danced on the pitch, and in the dressing-room a few minutes later tossed his boots into the air in sheer exuberance. The teams that day were:

Scotland: Dawson (Rangers); Carabine (Third Lanark), Cummings

(Aston Villa); Shankly (Preston N.E.), Baxter (Middlesbrough), McNab (West Bromwich Albion); McSpadyen (Partick Thistle), Walker (Hearts), Dougal (Preston N.E.), Venters (Rangers), Milne (Middlesbrough).

England: Woodley (Chelsea); Morris (Wolves), Hapgood (Arsenal); Willingham (Huddersfield Town), Cullis (Wolves), Mercer (Everton); Matthews (Stoke City), Hall, G. W. (Spurs), Lawton (Everton), Goulden (West Ham), Beasley (Huddersfield T.).

Two incidents I recall off the field were the Duke and Duchess of Gloucester facing the rain-storm, and seeing it through, and Mr. Brook Hirst's pep talk before the game. The chairman of the F.A. came into the dressing-room and gave this little speech: "Well, boys, I haven't come to tell you how to play, but I offer these words of advice. Man for man you are as good, if not better, than your opponents, but you will be handicapped to-day by the spirit and fire of a Scottish crowd. Everyone out there will be doing his bit to help Scotland win, but I believe you boys can win for England. So go out there, and never mind about that Hampden roar."

And so in blinding rain we went out and struggled for ninety minutes, but it was worth the soaking. We showed them we could overcome the Hampden bogy.

CHAPTER VIII

WOT! NO CARTILAGE?

A loose cartilage—and a freak cure. . . . A plane crash and fourteen head stitches. . . . Englishman plays for Wales. . . . Ted Robbins—sad and happy. . . . When Mortensen nearly hanged himself.

FREDDIE STEELE played part of a season with a loose cartilage. Well, Stanley Mortensen, Blackpool, stopped playing for weeks because he thought he had cartilage trouble. His "cure" was amazing. It all began when Stan injured his right knee playing for Blackpool against Rochdale in 1944. He visited four specialists over a period of some weeks, and after each consultation was advised to undergo an operation for the removal of a cartilage. Finally, he visited the M.O. at the R.A.F. camp where he was stationed as an air-gunner and wireless operator. The M.O. decided not to give Mortensen time off duty for the operation, but Stan was put in a lower medical grade, and excused marching, drilling and P.T. duties for four months.

And so the speedy young Blackpool forward—he was playing inside-left at this time—missed the last couple of months of the 1943–44 season. During the summer he played cricket for Blackpool Services, and impressed as a first-class wicket-keeper. The continual rising and bending helped to strengthen the injured knee, and when the 1944-45 football season came round, Mortensen consulted another specialist at Newcastle, who dashed any hopes Stan had, confirming the opinion of the other doctors, that there was cartilage trouble. His advice to Stan was that he should take a ball out and kick it hard. That would decide one way or the other.

It was "kill or cure." Stan thought this over, and did not have to wait long. On his first day back at Blackpool he was walking on the sands where a crowd of R.A.F. boys were kicking a football. Stan remembered the advice he had been given, and running up, took one great kick. The next moment he was doubled up in pain, believing he broken his leg.

The amazing sequel is that Mortensen has never been troubled with that leg since. He was soon back in the Blackpool team, and in a short time was up among the leading scorers. Yet four doctors had advised an operation. To-day Mortensen is playing centre-forward for Blackpool, and with great success. He has wonderful speed off the mark. Mortensen was spotted by Blackpool while playing for South Shields schoolboys at Blackpool. Joe Smith signed him as an amateur. Yet, strangely, he was not picked out as an international in the making until he began playing as a "guest" with Bath City, the non-League club, early in the war.

Mortensen can thank his lucky stars he is playing football at all to-day. On his last nine-hundred mile flight, before being posted to a squadron, the plane in which he was flying crashed into a forest near Lossiemouth in Scotland. The pilot and bomb-aimer were killed. The navigator lost a leg, and Mortensen had severe head injuries which called for fourteen stitches. Yet this enthusiast was out playing again three weeks after the accident. Only Stan Mortensen would attempt such a crazy stunt. He was convalescing at Newport, and took a Saturday afternoon off to watch the Welsh Cup Final between Lovell's Athletic and Swansea Town. Swansea arrived a player short. Mortensen could not resist the temptation, and volunteered to play at outside-right for Swansea, who won 4—2.

Not many weeks later he turned out for a Scottish Selected XI against the British Army at Aberdeen. Mortensen was the only Englishman in the Scottish team. He was picked as centre-forward, and found he was opposed by Stanley Cullis. Although the British team won 5—4, Stanley had the satisfaction of scoring all of Scotland's four goals. At one time Mortensen's ambition was to be a centre-forward. His wish came true, but I think Stan to-day is happy in an inside position. He has more room in which to move, and can still make his now famous dashes from " nowhere " down the middle.

Mortensen is one of the few English footballers who has played for Wales. His international debut was made *against* England! He had been chosen as England's reserve against Wales at Wembley on September 25, 1943. He was sitting on the touch-line with Bill Voisey, the English trainer, when Ivor Powell (Queen's Park Rangers), playing at left-half for Wales, fractured a collar-bone early in the game. Shortly after Powell was carried off, that grand old man of Welsh football, the late Mr. Ted Robbins, and Mr. Rous had a quick chat in the stand. Word was sent down to the touch-line, and Mortensen went trotting to the dressing-room. Nobody in the 80,000 crowd had any idea that Mortensen was going in to change, and when a quarter of an hour later the player in the red jersey returned on the field a cheer went up from the crowd who, not knowing the seriousness of Powell's injury, were under the impression the injured Welsh left-half was returning. Even when " Powell " went to inside-left and Ronnie Burgess ('Spurs) dropped back to left-half the onlookers did not suspect anything unusual, as team switches are often necessary after a player has been injured.

Even some of the England players did not know that Mortensen was playing on the other side and football reporters whose headquarters at Wembley are at the top of the main stand, did not know of the change until after half-time.

Such a substitution could not have been made in a full international—or in any League or Cup game, but the internationals played during the war do not go down in the records as full internationals. Neither did any of the players chosen for these war-time games receive " caps."

It was the only case of a substitute being allowed in a war-time international, but it was a wise move by Mr. Rous and Mr. Robbins to save the game from being too big a farce for the 80,000 who had paid to see a good match. As it was England won 8—3, and the lovable Ted Robbins was almost heartbroken, when I met him outside the England dressing-room: " I can take a licking, Stanley," he said, " but, honestly, my boys didn't play as badly as that score suggests." I was only too willing to endorse that statement, because the Welsh team had put up a much more spirited fight than the score suggested.

It was a far happier Mr. Robbins I met at Manchester three weeks later after England had defeated Scotland 8—0. The white-haired Welsh F.A. secretary nudged me in the ribs with elbow, and chuckled: "At least Wales cracked three past the England defence." He was happy again. Lost Welsh prestige had been restored by the pasting we had given Scotland.

It had been during the match against Wales that I was alleged to have been "starved" by the rest of the England team, and a controversy raged in the newspapers for some days afterwards, but more about that particular incident in a later chapter.

It would not be fitting to leave the adventures of Mortensen without telling how this descendant of Scandinavia—his grandfather was a Norwegian—nearly hanged himself! Not attempted suicide of course! While training as a member of a bomber crew he had to make practice parachute jumps. The enthusiastic footballing airman was almost strangled by the rip-cord of his own parachute. Yet within a short space he was playing for Bath City. It takes more than a loose cartilage, a plane crash and a "hanging" to keep Mortensen down.

CHAPTER IX

THE BOLTON DISASTER

Blackest Saturday. . . . The referee was correct. . . . My mind was on the game. . . . "It's a crime to carry on." . . . Depression next day.

THE most tragic match in which I ever played was the Bolton Wanderers—Stoke City cup-tie at Burnden Park, Bolton, on March 9, 1946, when thirty-three spectators were crushed to death and 500 injured as a result of several hundred gate-crashers squeezing into the Bolton ground. It was the blackest Saturday in the history of the game, and shocked a nation who after six years of war had begun to accept with dry eyes the deaths of children in air-raids, hospitals being bombed, and thousands of lives being lost at sea and in battle.

The previous great football disaster had occurred at Ibrox Park, Glasgow, in 1902 when during an England–Scotland international a stand collapsed killing twenty-five spectators and injuring hundreds of others. Looking back on this Bolton tragedy I am surprised the British public was so shocked coming so soon after the worst war in the world's history. Here was a war-toughened people distressed by thirty-three lives lost at a football game. The explanation, I suppose, is that we had no other choice than to be fatalistic during the war. Civilians as well as soldiers went from day to day uncertain whether they would see the sun rise next day. To survive a war, therefore, only to die at a football match sent a shiver running down the spine of nearly every one of us. At war we are a tough nation. At play we are sentimental and sympathetic.

It was for the families of the victims left behind that we mourned. Of the wife who had packed her man's lunch in order that he could finish work early and get to the cup-tie in time for the kick-off. How could she have realized this would be the last time she would see him alive? How could she break the news to her little ones?

There have been many hysterical words voiced and written about the tragedy at Bolton. Some believed it was scandalous to allow the game to continue while the dead were strewn with coats covering their crushed bodies. Mr. George Dutton, of Warwick, the referee, was criticized. Let me state right here that it was the only sensible decision to make. I would not like to have been the man responsible for the stopping of the game, as I have not the slightest doubt such action would have increased the casualties from hundreds to thousands.

It has been stated that thousands of fans realized immediately some of their colleagues had been killed in that first mad rush when the game was only twelve minutes old. My impression is that few of the crowd of nearly 70,000 were aware of the tragedy in their midst. I will go as far as to say that thousands left the ground happily unaware that lives had been lost.

Picture, therefore, the temper of a crowd that had fought and struggled for more than three hours, on being told the game was abandoned. It would have been a case of an excited mob believing they had been denied their rights. A riot might have followed before placards could have been prepared explaining exactly what had happened, and thousands of Cup crazy fans might have stampeded.

How did the players react? I can only answer for myself, but I believe I can speak for the other twenty-one when I say that within a few minutes of returning to the field after the hold up of twenty-six minutes we had forgotten the men, who a little earlier had been cheering us, were now lying dead. Some of them, no doubt, had been about to release a cheer when the stampede overtook them, and had died screaming for air.

I may be accused of hardness when I say our minds were soon on the game again, but it is the truth. For one thing we did not realize just how serious the disaster had been. Stoke City were two goals down from the previous Saturday's tie, and all the Stoke boys could think about was how to get on equal terms with Bolton.

Before this never-to-be-forgotten cup-tie began Bob McGrory had given us a " pep " talk in the dressing-room. " We're two down, lads," Bob explained in broad Scotch, " get out and throw yourselves into the game from the kick-off. By these methods we have nothing to lose, and everything to gain."

How right he was. If we could have scored an early goal I think we would have won this tie, and perhaps have gone on to Wembley for the first time in Stoke City's history. For although two goals down every member of our side had honestly believed we were going to pull the game off.

As we trotted on to the pitch I noticed the crowd was tightly packed, but this was nothing unusual at a big cup-tie. Our boys began well, and after ten minutes we had reason to feel confident as we were having the best of the game. It then happened! There was a terrific roar from the crowd, and I glanced over my shoulder to see thousands of fans coming from the terracing behind the far goal on to the pitch.

I did not take undue notice. After all, I have often seen a tightly-packed crowd free itself by invading the touch-lines for better vision and breathing conditions. Mr. Dutton blew his whistle to stop play, and hurried to the touch-line to ask the police to push some of the spectators back over the touch-line He came back, and the game continued after a bounce of the ball, but a few minutes later a police sergeant walked on to the pitch and spoke to the referee.

While Mr. Dutton and the sergeant talked, Tommy Woodward, Bolton's outside-left, strolled over to me and said solemnly: " They'll never get this game finished to-day, Stan." It was then the referee called the two captains, Neil Franklin of Stoke City and Harry Hubbick of Bolton, and explained a spectator had been killed in the crush, and it was advisable for us to retire to the dressing-rooms until complete order was restored.

As we walked off the field and through the tunnel that led to the dressing-rooms we were not aware how dreadful the accident had been. The tunnel was packed with spectators who obviously had not been able to see the game, and I recall vividly hearing a broad Lancashire voice saying: " Ee lad, but that was a quick first half."

We pushed through the crowd to our dressing-room, and five minutes later George Mountford, Billy Mould and Alex Ormston, who travelled to Bolton as reserves, brought us the news that two or three people had been killed. We sat around for twenty-six minutes before Mr. Dutton came in to tell us that the game was to be resumed following the advice of the Chief Constable of Bolton. I shrugged my shoulders, and stood up ready to go out again. I was just a footballer, and my duty obviously was to obey the referee, who was acting on expert advice. Returning through the tunnel, one

MATTHEWS THE BOY

At 11 when playing for Wellington Road School, Hanley

JACK MATTHEWS IN HIS PRIME

angry spectator, who realized part of the tragedy, caught hold of Frank Baker, outside-left, and shouted: "It's a crime to carry on."

Thousands of spectators had come to the touch-line, and a fresh line had been made with saw-dust, which meant we were now playing on a slightly smaller pitch. Once the game had been resumed, the player's main thought was of winning. Stoke had a big share of the play, but the ground was soggy, and our forwards, including myself, could not get set to put in a really dangerous shot.

The earlier incidents had been forgotten when the whistle blew for half-time. Yet as soon as play stopped my mind was worrying about the rumours we had heard in the dressing-room. We were ready to walk off, but Mr. Walter Rowley, Bolton's secretary-manager at that time, who was standing on the touch-line, shouted to the referee to carry on, and not to allow the players off. It was sound reasoning to turn straight round and continue. A ten-minute break might have had a depressing effect on the players, and on the section of the crowd who had heard about the deaths.

With the game resumed my only thoughts for the next forty-five minutes were that we were still two goals down, and that something had to be done if Stoke were to survive in the Cup. We battled on, and did everything but score. With only fifteen minutes remaining we were still enjoying much of the play, but the goals did not come. The nearest was when we struck the cross-bar with the Bolton goal-keeper beaten. The Stoke wing-halves worked overtime, and the forwards did not spare themselves. I roamed from the right wing to inside-left, but all in vain. It just was not our day.

When the final whistle blew we marched off realizing Stoke had been knocked out of the Cup. That was the chief tragedy of these fleeting seconds. In our dressing-room again we heard more rumours about the increasing number of casualties. Yet it was not until I was motoring to Blackpool that evening that the shadow of the grim disaster descended on me like a storm-cloud.

The shock next morning was even worse. I sat down to breakfast, but when I picked up a Sunday newspaper and read the tragic facts, I pushed the food before me aside and went to my room. I felt quite sick.

CHAPTER X

MY SECRET

Confidence. . . . Ball-control. . . . Fitness. . . . Quickness off the mark. . . . Beat an opponent close up. . . . Aim to centre for the far post. . . . Various tactics.

I HAVE often been asked to explain the secret of my success as a dribbler. It is a difficult request because whatever football ability I have came almost naturally to me. I do not wish to give a false impression by these words, because while there are some fans who enjoy watching me there are others who are stern critics of my style. Some say I am not a match-winner, and I have not the scoring capabilities of the late Alex Jackson, Cliff Bastin or Joe Hulme. Others say I do not get sufficiently " stuck in."

My reply to the first allegation is that I always try to play pure football, to confuse the opposing defence, and then make an opening by which a colleague in a more suitable scoring position than myself may finish off the movement. To the second allegation I say firmly, that if my career had depended on just how well I could get " stuck in ", I would have retired from football many years ago. The science of football is to beat your opponent by superior skill, speed or tactics. The player who chooses to stoop to tripping, ankle-tapping or follow through with his boot after he has tackled is admitting he has not the craft to meet the opposition on equal and legitimate terms.

I hope I shall not be accused of boasting when I say dribbling came naturally to me. I did, of course, practise for hours on end as a kid kicking that rubber ball against our garden wall.

To dribble successfully the most essential factor is supreme confidence to beat an opponent. If I even entertained the possibilty that I am going to lose the ball when I am tackled I would be a failure. I know I am going to beat the half-back or full-back, or both, standing in front of me. If I can " show " the man tackling me the ball by taking it close to him, and then whip it past him, causing him to lunge, when he thinks he has cornered me, I will soon have caused an inferiority complex from which my opponent will not easily recover. A successful dribbler must develop a superiority complex in his own mind.

Next to confidence I rely on ball-control, fitness, an easy feinting trick, and a natural swerve. What of speed? Speed as a rule is not essential to be a successful dribbler. The requirement is quickness off the mark, and for this I suggest the would-be dribbler should practise sprinting laps of twenty yards. This method is part of my training, because if I can outsprint my opponent to the ball I am confident I can outwit him once the ball is at my feet.

If a back is running alongside me one of my favourite tricks is to make him run in the wrong direction by turning my right foot in, and causing him to believe I am going to turn to his right. This movement is usually sufficient to cause the back to hesitate for a split second, but without stopping I push the ball forward with my *left instep,* and if all goes well I should be clear.

Eddie Hapgood once said I dribble for the sake of dribbling, and am not content to beat a man once. Eddie thinks I like to beat the same opponent several times to demonstrate my skill to the crowd. This is not true. I dribble to get on top of the defence, hoping to destroy the confidence of my opponents. Once I have the opposition in two minds, the path is clear to make openings for my own colleagues.

To those critics who cannot understand why I do not cut in and score more goals my answer is that as a young player I did cut in, and I did score goals. I was so enthusiastic to make good at Stoke that my one aim was to get as many goals as possible, and at one period I was among the club's leading scorers. But then I thought to myself that a winger who could make scoring openings for the centre-forward and inside-men would be of greater value to the team than the winger who wants to do the scoring himself.

So I concentrated on dribbling in such a way that it would throw the opposing defence out of gear. To perfect this I spent many many weeks practising with a ball at my feet, and stakes in the ground. The stakes, of course, were imaginary opponents, and although it was easy to dribble round these " dead men " knowing they could not tackle, I am convinced that my spell among the sticks served me admirably later in my career.

Another important rule for a winger to remember is to aim to centre to the far post. This tip sounds simple enough, but many wingers forget its importance. I shall never forget the day these words of Soccer wisdom were passed on to me. I was sitting in the Stoke dressing-room, a mere lad of sixteen, when Billy Meredith, the old Welsh wizard, and acclaimed by old timers as the greatest of all wingers, approached me and said: " You show promise of becoming a good 'un, lad. Don't lose your head, and remember to place your centre for the far post. Another thing, lad, always listen to men older than yourself. You may have to listen to a little nonsense, but if you sift the good from the bad, you'll learn much. Listening is the cheapest form of education."

With these words of wisdom, the great Meredith, who gained

fifty-one international " caps " for Wales, left me deep in thought. I have not forgotten his advice, and right now I am still listening—and still learning.

Every footballer has one or two secrets. One of my favourite tricks is to take the ball down the wing, close to the touch-line, and when challenged by the back, instead of turning in towards the goal, I flick the ball with my right foot to his left, and then sprint past him. Here I must emphasize the secret of success lies almost entirely in timing. It is essential to hold on to the ball until the last possible split-second before the back comes at you.

I think I can speak for most wingers when I say the wing forward likes the back to come at him. However, there is not any need to be alarmed when faced by a back who does not tackle at once, but waits for the winger to make the first mistake. In this case the best plan is to take the ball up to him—right under his nose. All that is left for him to do is to make a desperate late tackle. When you get a back in this state, the rest should be simple.

This move requires years of practice before it is perfected. The inexperienced winger who attempts to hang on to the ball will find himself quickly dispossessed. However, once the winger masters this trick he will find it invaluable when attempting to beat an opponent.

The next move is to take the ball well down towards the goal—sometimes to within a few feet of the goal-line. This may start my critics screaming. I am sometimes accused of wasting time and giving the opposing defence plenty of time to get into position, but my answer is that from this position it is impossible to make an off-side pass. Think back on how many wing break-aways are cut short by an off-side pass. This is a much more serious offence than allowing the defence a few seconds to get into position, because the forward who does not study the position of his colleagues before passing is throwing away the advantage to his own side by conceding a free kick that might lead to a goal against his own team.

Another tip worth remembering is for a winger to be ready for a break-away at all times—even when his own colleagues are being pushed well and truly into their own half, and especially when his own team is defending a corner kick. Too many wingers stand out on the touch-line as though it is none of their business when a corner is being taken. This is bad team work, because forwards can help defence, and backs can help forwards. One of the best examples of what a defender can do to assist his attack was Frank Swift, the former Manchester City and England goalkeeper. Those who have seen Big Frank in action will know what I mean. He never took a wild kick at the ball to show the crowd how far he could kick.

it. Instead he threw it to the feet of a half-back or an inside-forward who immediately was on the attack. That is much better than placing a high-powered kick at the feet of an opposing half-back. Of course, Frank is such a splendid physical specimen that he found it easier to throw a ball over his right shoulder than the average goalkeeper, but I notice more and more keepers are following Swift's profitable " goal-throw."

Now about a winger's duty when a corner kick is being taken against his own side. I have found it pays dividends to stroll into an inside position. Nine out of ten loose balls come at you in this position, and without an opponent standing on top of you it is possible to turn a defensive movement into sudden attack—sometimes ending in a break-away goal.

Freddie Steele and I had this understanding when I was at Stoke, and many a time it proved a match winner. It was the plan Arsenal exploited so often when they were almost unbeatable, and became known as the " Bank of England " team. How many times in the past do you remember reading of Arsenal being pressed into their own half for most of the game, only to score the winning goal by a smash-and-grab raid? Supporters of the opposite side always chanted " Lucky Arsenal " but I do not agree with them. Tactics are most important in football, and if a team can plan to win an important game by such methods I say " Good luck " to them.

Keenness in football is essential, but keenness must not be misinterpreted. I have no time for that " get stuck in " policy that is sometimes advised in cup-ties or local derbys. Once one side starts tackling with too much vigour there is inevitable retaliation and loss of tempers.

Fortunately, the Football Association, who have kept the sport they govern cleaner than any other sport in the world, do not encourage this type of player, and the footballer, no matter how good he may be, realizes he will not play for England if he chooses to adopt these methods. If the Football Association was not so strict I have not the slightest doubt that professional football would have been ruined many, many years ago.

A perfect example of what can happen if one side becomes over-vigorous is the England-Italy game at Highbury in 1934 about which I talked in an earlier chapter chapter. If I had to get "stuck in " I should never kick another football as long as I live. Happily, there are not many serious offenders in the game. Most footballers are thorough sportsmen, and respect the code of fair-play. So whatever my young readers may be learning about Soccer, don't allow anybody to persuade you to play the rough stuff. It does not pay in the long run.

CHAPTER XI

AN ENGLAND RECORD

Down with 'flu. . . . "Doc" Voisey. . . . Bert Brown—ballerina. . . . Billy Wright's first game for England. . . . Luminous flags and a white fog. . . . Delayed-action pills.

FEW of the eighty-five thousand spectators who saw me make my forty-fourth appearance for England against Belgium at Wembley on January 19, 1946, and so break Eddie Hapgood's international record, could have realized how close I came to missing that game. If I had cried off, Hapgood's record would have stood for nearly a year longer because a knee injury kept me out of the England team to play Scotland at Hampden Park the following April, and I had to drop out again after being selected to play for England in the first two international games in the 1946–47 season, again owing to a knee injury.

Prior to the match against Belgium I had been on night duty with the R.A.F. It was during a bitterly cold spell, and my duties involved turning out of bed at all hours of the night and morning. By the Thursday before the international I had caught a really bad cold, but hoped to fight off the germs by dosing myself at night with hot milk and whisky.

I left Blackpool on the Friday morning reasonably fit, but after being in the train an hour I began to feel desperately ill. My breathing became difficult, my head began to swim, and I came close to passing out on more than one occasion. In fact, a friend who travelled with me from Blackpool was so alarmed he suggested on my arrival in London I should make immediately for St. Mary's Hospital to a doctor friend and get an injection to combat what was now obviously a severe attack of influenza.

I could not eat the sandwiches my wife had packed, and long before we were due in London I was convinced that I would not, after all, be breaking the record of appearances for England. My spirits were low when I stepped off the train at Euston, but after a brief walk and a welcome puff of fresh air after more than five hours in a stuffy train I felt a little better and decided I would go to the hotel where the team was staying, and get to bed.

Kindly Bill Voisey, the England trainer, was taken aback when he saw me stagger through the lounge, and peer at him through eyes half closed with the 'flu that had now well and truly got hold of me.

"You look a bit dicky," said the likeable Bill with some alarm in his tone. "What have you been doing with yourself, Stan?"

"Just a bit of a cold, Bill," I replied, "I'll get to bed, and I'll be fit to-morrow."

"Just a bit of a cold!" growled Bill; "I should say so! Laddie, you've got the 'flu, and you and I have got quite a fight on if we're going to give the germs the k.o. Up to bed, Stan, and I'll get you a drop of something to make you sweat."

With that the England trainer left me, and I lifted my aching limbs slowly up the stairs to my room. It was a wonderful feeling to get between the sheets. Bill was as good as his word, and I woke after a doze to find him standing beside my bed with a glass of hot milk in his hand.

"Here, Stan," he said, "Take this. I've managed to get you a drop of medicine that will do the trick."

Bill's "medicine" was a stiff dose of whisky. I slept again, and woke to find my pyjamas wet with perspiration. Bill Voisey fussed round me that night like a hen nursing a sickly chick back to health. Nothing was too much bother for him. I had dinner in bed, and Bill stayed in my room telling me stories of the old-timers.

Bill is something of a psychologist, and figured that if left to my own depression my chances of playing next day would be small. So he aimed to keep me as cheerful as possible. As ill as I felt I must confess the England trainer had me in a good humour that night. Bill Voisey is one of the best team-men I have ever known. He has built himself around the virtue of loyalty. Whether is was Millwall, Fulham or England he was serving you could depend on him to give himself 100 per cent to the task.

Few people realize Bill had a wonderful war record. The reason for this is that Bill never talks about himself. In the 1914–18 war he served as a sergeant in the R.F.A., and spent three years in the Flanders trenches. His cheerfulness and his gallantry made him loved by those around him, and won him the Distinguished Conduct Medal, the Military Medal and the Croix de Guerre. I have never ever heard Voisey mention how he won these medals. In the second world war, Bill insisted on doing his bit for England as always, and joined the Home Guard. He served throughout the blitz on London. —Voisey probably served Millwall better than any one man has served any club in Great Britain. For forty-five years he has been connected with the club as a programme-boy, player, trainer and manager during the second war. Millwall played on the Isle of Dogs when Bill first sold programmes. Later he played for them for sixteen years, and became a really first-class wing half-back. He was nick-named "Banger" Voisey by the supporters. But all through his career, whether as player, trainer, manager or scout, he was also a friend and an optimist. That is why he is respected by all who have been connected with him.

He was certainly more than just a trainer to me the night I was ill. Before it was time to turn out the lights he insisted on giving me a good rub down. Then he tucked me in, and with a reassuring wink bade me *au revoir*. I had a good night's sleep, and woke up much better in the morning apart from the fact that my throat was very sore. I had no idea how much trouble my cold had caused until the England trainer came into my room to see how his patient had fared after "Doc" Voisey's prescription of the previous night, whisky, milk, common sense and determination to keep the patient happy.

The football reporters began ringing to know whether I would play or whether I would have to postpone the smashing of Hapgood's forty-three appearances for England.

"What shall I tell 'em?" asked Bill.

"Tell them I'm playing," I whispered, because when I tried to shout I found I could scarcely make the England trainer hear me. I can say now in all honesty that I doubt if I could have dragged myself from the bed had it not been for the record, because I was far from well, but it was such an occasion I felt I could not miss this game.

I had breakfast in bed, another rub-down from Voisey, and was as fit as I could possibly be under the circumstances. I wrapped up well, and with a scarf round my throat was driven to Wembley in a taxi chartered by the Football Association.

There were 85,000 fans packed into Wembley on this bleak January day, and the snow that had fallen previously had not entirely disappeared from the pitch. The England team were handed special track suits—blouses and long trousers of sky-blue. Some of us felt a little bit self-conscious about appearing before our own spectators, and Bert Brown of Charlton, who was later transferred to Nottingham Forest and then Aston Villa, and then took over as manager of Gorleston, caused great amusement in the dressing-room by doing an imitation of a ballet dancer.

The Belgians did not wear track-suits. This brought some criticism from the press, who pointed out that it was a little thoughtless to leave the Belgians shivering while the English players were well wrapped up. Mr. Rous explained the position clearly enough by pointing out that although the England team had not worn these track-suits before they had been in store at the Football Association offices for some years. It was not the F.A.'s job to supply visiting teams with track-suits, he explained. When an England team visited a foreign country the F.A. did not expect to be supplied with equipment.

I was glad to wear a track suit in view of my cold—especially as the players are kept hanging about longer on these special occasions than in ordinary League games. We lined up to be introduced to the Prime Minister, Mr. Clement Attlee, by Joe Mercer, the captain, and then took off our suits to begin the game.

I should perhaps point out that while I was the doubtful starter for the game it was Frankie Soo who had to pull out shortly before the match owing to a twisted knee muscle. This situation gave Jesse Pye of Notts County, now with Wolves, the chance to make his first appearance for England.

Young Billy Wright of Wolves had originally been chosen as inside-left to partner his club colleague, Jimmy Mullen. The selectors decided to put Wright in Soo's place at right-half, switch Bert Brown from inside-right to inside-left, and make Pye my partner on the right wing. The final line-up of the England team was:

Swift (Manchester City); Scott (Arsenal), Hardwick (Middlesbrough;) Wright (Wolves), Franklin (Stoke City), Mercer (Everton); (captain); Matthews (Stoke), Pye (Notts County), Lawton (Chelsea), Brown (Charlton), Mullen (Wolves).

It is rather odd that Billy Wright was again chosen at inside-left for England nearly six years later after he had established himself as captain and as either the right- or left-half. It is also odd that he did not play in the forward line owing to injury.

The second time Billy was chosen as England's inside-left was against Austria at Wembley in November 1951. The Austrians had been boosted as the champions of Europe, and as recent England teams had been severely criticized by the football writers prior to the match with Austria, the F.A. selectors took the bold step of transferring Wright from his consolidated position in the half-back line to inside-forward in an attempt to bring stability and goals.

Was this a wise move? Some thought so, and many disagreed. Personally, I consider Wright a far more effective wing half-back than an inside-forward. Certainly Mr. J. S. Baker, Wolves chairman, was annoyed that Billy was chosen for a position in the England team which conflicted with his normal place in the Wolves eleven. He voiced his protest publicly.

Anyway, fate stepped in again, because although Billy played inside-forward in the practice games at Manchester, an injury to Billy Nicholson, the Spurs right-half, also chosen in the England half-back line, caused Nicholson to withdraw, and Wright was then switched to right-half. So twice in six years Billy Wright was chosen as an inside-forward for England, but never played in that position on either occasion.

It was not a great game, and although we won 2–0, I think the crowd were a little disappointed, but for myself I must say I enjoyed it because I forgot about my cold. I think Frank Swift will agree with me when I say that never before had England's gigantic goalkeeper had such a quiet afternoon. On the other hand François Daenen, the dapper five feet six inches Belgian goalkeeper, was kept well and truly warm from a succession of shots from Tommy Lawton and Co. What surprised me was the manner in which Daenen could get to the high balls. Perhaps he had the same uncanny gift as the great Harry Hibbs (Birmingham), who was only five feet six inches tall.

Considering the conditions under which I played I was satisfied with my performance. It would not be fair or fitting for me to pass comment on my play, but perhaps I will be excused for quoting the Belgian captain, Joe Poverick, who declared after the game: Matthews and Brown are the best forwards I have played against." That was generous praise from the veteran Belgian left-back, because he played exceptionally well, and I found him more difficult to beat than many other left-backs who boast that I am one of the easiest wingers in the world to handle.

Jesse Pye is a good player, he has the right temperament, because after missing an open goal in the first few minutes—an incident capable of ruining many players in their first international appearance—he settled down like an old campaigner. Bert Brown put us in front after thirteen minutes. Billy Wright brought off a long throw-in twelve yards inside the Belgian half, and with the opposition too amazed to move, Brown zig-zagged past Pannaye, the right-back, and left Daenen without a chance from a distance of twenty yards.

Ten minutes later Pye scored. He began the move himself, sending the ball out to where I was standing some forty yards from goal. I took it past Pannaye, to within two yards of the goal-line, and made a backwards pass that hovered above the goal area. Tommy Lawton went up to head it, but was inches short. The ball went on to Pye, standing about three yards behind Lawton, and about twelve yards from goal. The Notts County inside-forward steadied himself and shot hard. The Belgian goalkeeper had been distracted by Lawton's attempt to head the ball and did not move as Pye's shot sailed high into the back of the net.

After this it was all England, and the white fog that descended like a curtain at half-time must have ruined the game as far as the spectators were concerned. The players could just about see the ball and each other, which was more than we had been able to boast of when

I played as a guest in the Arsenal team that played the Moscow Dynamos at Tottenham in the previous November.

The only good this second-half fog did at Wembley was to show up the luminous flags used by the linesmen. This idea was adopted from the Russians, and was one of the points the members of the Dynamo party had discussed at the conference between English and Russian officials at the Football Association offices.

The idea is good, because in England there are often misty and dull days that are not bad enough to destroy the vision of play, but make it difficult for the referee, and spectators on the far side of the field, to see the linesmen's flags. Much booing and hooting might be avoided by the use of the luminous flag.

After the game there was a banquet in the evening, but I felt too ill to attend. The fog had not helped my 'flu, and now the excitement was over I felt ill again. In fact, I was not able to eat anything, and retired to bed within a couple of hours of the finish of the match.

I could hardly speak on the Sunday morning, and was thoroughly miserable on my journey back to Blackpool. Depression set in, and I spent the next four days in bed. It was not until the following Friday that I began to feel a little better. Stoke City had an important cup-tie against Sheffield United. I reported to the Stoke ground on Saturday morning, and told Bob McGrory I was not fit; that my legs were weak, and I did not think I had the stamina to last out for ninety minutes.

Bob seemed worried, and telephoned a specialist at the Royal Infirmary, and asked if he could prescribe something to give me the necessary stamina. The specialist gave me two capsules which he described as pep pills used by members of the Luftwaffe before taking off to raid England during the war. I was told to take the pills an hour before the kick-off.

I did as instructed, and am satisfied they gave me the necessary stamina to pull through and help Stoke City beat Sheffield United, but the after-effects were extraordinary. About nine o'clock that night I was feeling somewhat tired after the game, and was dozing in an arm-chair when suddenly I became wide awake. It was just as though something inside me was determined I should get out of my chair. I felt so keyed-up that I had to leave my chair and pace up and down the room. I would willingly have gone out and played a game of football there and then. If I never knew before, I certainly learned then the meaning of delayed action!

CHAPTER XII

HAPPY ORDEAL

Injured at Blackpool. . . . I am honoured at Stoke. . . . My first speech.

WHAT was the toughest moment of my career? Losing my place in the England team after the Italian match at Highbury? playing second fiddle to Switzerland's dance-band leader at Zurich in 1938? When Stoke City suggested I should play in the reserves? Or, playing with influenza against the Belgians? All of these were tough enough, but the tightest corner I have ever been in was not on a football pitch, but in the Stoke City Town Hall, when the Lord Mayor of Stoke, Mr. Percy Williams, presented me with an illuminated address in recognition of my forty-four appearances for England.

This may sound silly, but the reason this presentation became an ordeal for me was that I was warned beforehand I would have to make a speech. Ask me to oppose the cleverest back in football. Ask me to try my golf luck against Henry Cotton, the prince of golfers. Ask me to oppose Budge at tennis. Any of these tall orders would not worry me, because I could only be beaten, but I am no speaker, and the thought of giving a speech in the Town Hall was enough to twist my stomach into a thousand knots.

The presentation was fixed for 28th March, 1946, and I appreciated the great honour bestowed on me because the only other sportsmen who were presented with similar addresses by the Stoke Council were Lievers and Wainwright, the wonder swimmers. The previous afternoon Bob McGrory had given Blackpool permission to play me in the League game against Manchester United at Blackpool. I had hardly kicked the ball before I was put out of action when attempting to block a pass with my left foot, I felt a sickening pain shoot from my knee down my leg. I had to go off the field, and my heart sank into my boots because I suspected I had torn the ligaments of my knee.

Never before had I felt such pain, yet it is strange that the first thought that flashed through my anxious mind was Hampden Park. Would this injury keep me out of the England team to play Scotland the following month? Why I should think of this so quickly I do not know, because it is not possible to judge the extent of an injury of this kind for a day or so. Perhaps the reason for my pessimistic hunch was that only once before in my career had I been forced to leave the field through injury.

The knee was strapped up, and I returned to Betty with a long face. Hampden a fortnight off, a journey to Stoke next day plus the thought of making a speech! My wife suggested we should go over-night and that I should show the injury to a manipulative surgeon in Stoke who has a reputation of working "miracles" with his hands. So after a meal and a pot of tea my spirits rose, and the world seemed less glum to me. After the treatment, I still had the task of preparing my reply to the Lord Mayor next day. What could I say? After all, football is my profession.

If my livelihood depended upon my ability to talk, my wife and family would be starving to-day. Of one thing I was confident. The shorter the speech the more popular I would be, because I know what it is to be bored by the man who never knows when to dry up. If it had been a question of writing the reply I would not have been unduly disturbed, but it was the thought of standing in the crowded Council Chambers that made my knees rattle like castanets. Yet if it had been a question of appearing on a football pitch before a crowd of a few hundred thousand, it would not have taken me more than a few minutes to get to sleep the night before.

Next morning I found my knee stiff and sore, but it certainly was not any worse, and the swelling had not developed. I drove round to the Victoria Ground to report my injury to the Stoke manager, and from then I drove to keep a luncheon date with the City Councillors.

At two o'clock the presentation began. Nearly a hundred people were in the Chambers, and Betty, my mother, and my daughter Jean sat close at hand. The odd part was that in spite of my nervous-ness I found myself amused by the expression on my daughter's face as she stared fascinated—not by the illuminated address, but by the Lord Mayor's chains. There were, of course, many speeches, and occasionally my thoughts were miles away. Once I was back in my father's little shop in Hanley. I thought of dad a great deal, and I wished he could have been in the Chambers for this ceremony. How proud he would have been! The speeches were, of course, too flattering to be repeated in this book, but I am grateful to the Lord Mayor and the Councillors for their kindness, and I shall always endeavour to live up to the standard they set me.

When the speeches were over it was my turn to take the platform. It is odd that as the moment I had dreaded for some days arrived, I forgot my shyness. I felt among friends, and the words flowed freely. I was told afterwards I appeared to be overcome. If so it was not from my nervousness, but from the kindness that had been shown me. It was an ordeal, but the happiest ordeal of my career.

CHAPTER XIII

LIGAMENTS AND LINIMENT

An overdose. . . . I call off the Hampden game. . . . Sprinting in an hotel corridor. . . . England beaten in last thirty seconds. . . . Joe Mercer's injury. . . . Jimmy Delaney—at a premium.

A BOTTLE of liniment broke my long run of appearances for England. When I returned from the presentation ceremony at Stoke to Blackpool I was determined to do everything in my power to get my damaged knee fit for the great tussle against Scotland at Hampden Park. I had two weeks in which to do the trick. From Stoke I brought a bottle of liniment which I was told to apply several times a day. I am afraid my enthusiasm was too great because I overdosed my knee, with the result that I burned the flesh and caused severe inflammation. When I realized what had happened I was heart-broken because it meant the loss of eight precious days which should have been spent strengthening the damaged ligaments. All I could now do was bathe the swelling with hot fomentations—and this I did all day.

What was even more sickening was the fact that up to the time of the application of the liniment my chances of representing England for the forty-fifth time were bright. Alan Ure, the old Blackpool trainer, and Johnny Lynas, the present trainer, had worked hard to get me fit. I had taken long walks along the promenade, and the leg was standing up pretty well apart from a stiffness which made it difficult for me to bend my left leg, but the impression of the trainers was that they could get the leg loosened up in time for Hampden. I was quietly confident all would be well. Then the catastrophe. It would have been less aggravating had I been crocked, and had known I had no chance of playing, but to be put out of the England team through a bottle of liniment is something of a football tragedy.

In my heart I knew I was out, but as black as the prospects seemed I was determined to make a desperate attempt to get well in the week that remained, so I packed my bags and motored over to Stoke to see what the next four days would bring. Doctor Spark, the club doctor, and Hughie Nuthall, the trainer, did everything possible for me, but the most important treatment was the application of hot formentations.

All the time this was going on my knee seemed to be stiffening, so in the evenings I went walking, and spent much time on the rowing-machine in an attempt to loosen up the stiffness. On the Thursday before the Hampden game I decided to have a final test at the Stoke ground, and in spite of the optimism of Hughie Nuthall two days previously I knew I was licked when with the first kick at a ball I felt a sharp pain shoot down my leg. I continued kicking and twisting, but the leg was not strong enough. If only I had not lost those eight days! I suppose I could have got by, but it would have been a grave injustice to my colleagues to have taken the risk of breaking down. Hampden is an ordeal even for eleven fit Englishmen. It would be heart-breaking for only ten, but it was with a heavy heart I informed the Football Association I was a non-starter in the Hampden Stakes.

Billy Elliott, W.B.A., outside right, now with Burnley, who had been selected as my deputy when the team had been announced, thus stepped into his first Hampden. This was not Billy's international debut, however, because he had taken my place in the England side against Wales at Cardiff a couple of years previously when Blackpool made a successful request to the F.A. to release me from international duty in order that I might assist Blackpool against Aston Villa in the Football League North Cup Final.

I was now out of the England team, but I was determined not to miss Hampden, and on the Friday I motored with two friends to Glasgow. I found the folk in Scotland really marvellous. Every Scot wanted to see a long overdue football win over England as much as they had wanted to see Hitler beaten in the war, but they were all sympathetic. I have many friends in Scotland. My wife and father-in-law are Scotch, but I am never caught in two minds as to which side I would cheer for. I am 100 per cent behind England, and I was hoping for a great win this time.

Welcome visitor to my hotel was Mr. Jimmy Davies, manager of Greenock Morton, who kept a promise made months earlier by handing me six tickets for the match. Those who have tried to obtain tickets for Hampden or Wembley will appreciate it when I say chunks of gold would be ignored if tickets were to be had instead. In Glasgow this night some desperate Scottish businessmen were prepared to pay £25 for two guinea seats, and they couldn't get them even at this ridiculous price. Perhaps the luckiest man in Glasgow that night was the young man who came up to me, and explained he was at one time stationed with me in the R.A.F. at Blackpool. He had taken a chance of coming to Scotland without a ticket. I could not recall having known him, but his face was familiar, so I handed him one of the tickets. Anyone who follows England to Scotland without a ticket, and hopes to get in to see the match, deserves to see a "miracle" worked.

Few people in Glasgow that night would have believed that at eight o'clock I was sprinting up and down a corridor of my hotel. Mr.

George Max, then a director of Millwall F.C., and an osteopath, had come up with the Millwall party of directors, who never miss the Hampden game. He said he could get me fit in time for the match next day. I explained this could not be for two reasons. Firstly, I knew my leg would not stand up, and secondly Billy Elliott was now in the team. I had handed him the two tickets the F.A. allot each player, and whatever happened now I would not spring a disappointment on him.

However, Mr. Max insisted he should have a look at my injury, and so with Jimmy Davies I went to Mr. Max's bedroom. There I stretched on the bed while he pushed my left leg backwards and forwards, finally cracking my leg back with such force that I let out a gasp of pain. For half a minute afterwards I thought my leg had been broken, but as the pain lessened it seemed my leg had loosened a little, and when I put both my feet on the floor I found I could bend my knee far more freely than before. I have already stated I had made my mind up that whatever happened I would not be the cause for a disappointing blow to Elliott. As it happened I would not have been fit to play because as the night went on my injured knee became stiffer and became quite painful. This, no doubt, was due to the exertion put on it, and although it felt much better in the morning it was a long way from being sound.

In the Hampden stand I sat close to Messrs. Jack Tinn, the then manager of Portsmouth, George Allison, who was the Arsenal boss, and David Jack, Middlesbrough manager until last season. Sitting in the Press seats working for various newspapers were half-a-dozen ex-international footballers—Alex James, Eddie Hapgood, Tommy Muirhead, Andy Cuningham and David Meiklejohn.

Although there had been a slight shower in the morning the sun shone brightly as a mild burst of cheering told us the England team was coming out, led by the captain, Joe Mercer. A deafening roar confirmed that Scotland was only just behind. For those who will want to refresh their memory of this game, I am giving the teams:

Scotland: R. Brown (Queen's Park), Shaw (D.) (Hibernian), Shaw (J.) (Rangers) (captain), Campbell (Morton), Brennan (Airdrie), Husband (Partick Thistle), Waddell (Rangers), Dougal (Birmingham City), Delaney (Manchester United), Hamilton (Aberdeen), Liddell (Liverpool).

England: Swift (Manchester City), Scott (Arsenal), Hardwick (Middlesbrough), Wright (Wolverhampton Wanderers), Franklin (Stoke City), Mercer (Everton) (captain), Elliott (West Bromwich Albion), Shackleton (Bradford), Lawton (Chelsea), Hagan (Sheffield United), D. Compton (Arsenal).

JACK MATTHEWS IN LATER YEARS

PROTEST MEETING

Three thousand Stoke supporters attend Protest Meeting following request to be put on the transfer list in 1938

This was not England's day, because Scotland won for the first time in four years with the only goal of the match, scored by Jimmy Delaney, Scotland's centre-forward, in the last thirty seconds. Thousands of Scotsmen never even saw the goal, as they had left Hampden cursing the luck of the English, and taking it for granted that the result was a goalless draw. But the victory roar from more than 135,000 remaining Scots must have been heard a mile away. The cheer will certainly remain in my memory for many years to come.

It was a disappointing game for England, because a gallant and overworked defence had held on to within seconds of the finish, but in fairness the result only did justice to Scotland. They were the faster and more fiery side, and it was certainly the best Scottish team I had seen since just before the war. There was much severe criticism from the sports writers against the display by the England team, but in fairness to my colleagues I maintain that a team is only as good as the opposition allows it to be. Believe me, Scotland did not allow England any time to settle down that day. In fact, I consider they really won the game in the first five minutes, although the goal was scored in the last half minute.

The Scots began at a killing pace. With the Hampden roar behind them they opened with a five minutes' blitzkrieg on the England goal. How Swift, Scott, Hardwick, Franklin and Mercer kept the Scottish forwards out is beyond me. Our defence wavered several times, but never snapped. Yet, unlike the majority of war-time internationals, the real football moves came from Scotland, who played with understanding.

No doubt, the decision of the Scottish F.A. to call the players together a couple of days before the match had had successful results. Previously, Scottish players had not met each other until they arrived in the dressing-room at Hampden Park. This time they stayed in pleasant surroundings a few miles outside of Glasgow. In addition to playing golf, there were special talks on tactics. The hotel was guarded against intruders, and the well-meaning but very often disturbing autograph hunters were kept out. I find on the eve of internationals that the many callers who say they have met you at such-and-such a place are apt to be disturbing. I think every player will endorse this opinion. Worse than the actual match are the hours of waiting in the hotel beforehand.

Scotland won on their merits, but the facts are that but for two cruel twists of fate Tommy Lawton must have made England almost sure winners before half-time. In the first fifteen minutes, Tommy had atrocious luck when Denis Compton sent across a square pass, and the Chelsea centre-forward banged the ball from thirty yards out. When Lawton really hits a ball I don't think there is a goalkeeper in the world who can do much about it. Bobby Brown was completely beaten, but the ball struck the cross-bar and rebounded into play to be quickly cleared by Husband, Scotland's left-half. You could hear the groan of nearly 140,000 Scotsmen, followed by the sigh of relief as the cross-bar came to the rescue. Not long afterwards Tommy Lawton again had to watch a piece of wood rob him of what appeared to be a certain goal. Elliott slipped round Jock Shaw and centred across the goalmouth.

Up went Tommy Lawton to Elliott's centre, and with a jerk of his head sent the ball to Brown's right. Bobby could not get there, and left it, the ball struck the foot of the post, and rolled round, and over the line into safety. Scotland breathed again.

Either of these Lawton attempts might have won the game, and a goal when things are going badly is the finest tonic any football team could have. The inferiority complex goes, and it is on the cards that if England had scored in this match at Hampden they would have settled down to play exhibition football.

I am not a believer in excuses because nothing can alter the result in the record books, but it must not be overlooked that Joe Mercer injured his left knee in the first few minutes, and instead of the usual polished display expected from Joe, he was often struggling. Joe could hardly walk next day, and as he had suspected he had a spot of cartilage trouble. In view of this big handicap it was a truly great performance to stick it out for nearly ninety minutes.

Billy Wright (Wolves) consolidated his place in the England team in this game. He was the youngest player on the field, but showed all the confidence of a veteran. Of course, we were all disappointed about the result, but there were many of us who realized it was a good thing for football for the victories to go round. Scotland had had to put up with a long run of defeats, and in many senses it was good to see that the team had regained the traditional fire and fighting spirit that seemed to be lacking during the war years. Outstanding success was Frank Brennan, the 22-year-old Airdrie centre-half, who stands 6 feet 2 inches, and who was playing in his first international. Brennan was not the original choice to hold Tommy Lawton, but when Young, the Glasgow Rangers' centre-half, cried off, the Scottish selectors took a chance with youth. The gamble came off because Frank began with remarkable coolness against Lawton, and Tommy will be the first to endorse my statement that Brennan is a good player.

At the end of the 1945–46 season Brennan crossed the border to join Newcastle United, and helped to get them back into the First Division after fourteen years in the Second Division.

Another Scot who had a good debut in international football was

Neil Dougal, the Birmingham inside-right and son of Willie Dougal, the Burnley trainer. Yet the man who really inspired his side was Manchester United's Jimmy Delaney at centre forward. It will be recalled that for many years when Jimmy was playing with Celtic he was excluded from internationals because of the story of his brittle bones. He had had an unlucky run of fractures with the result that a very high premium was asked of the Scottish F.A. to insure him against injury in international games. The Scottish officials decided not to take the risk, and Jimmy was excluded.

When Scotland were so often beaten by England during the war a well-known football writer began a "Bring Back Delaney" campaign with the result that an insurance company volunteered to accept the Delaney risk. This was lucky for Scotland, because in this match he crowned a fine afternoon's work by tapping in the all important winning goal just as the referee was glancing at his watch to end the game. Jimmy keeps on disturbing full-backs, and returned to his native land when Manchester United transferred him to Aberdeen.

It was tough on our boys who had struggled gamely for ninety minutes, but the better team had won.

CHAPTER XIV

THE FIRST LISBON STORY

Oranges and bananas. . . . We lose at roulette. . . . Hobbis talks Englishio. . . . Police charge with drawn swords. . . . Nick-named Mateus. . . . "We are from Stoke." . . . Portuguese hospitality.

ONE of the most enjoyable trips I have had in my footballing career was with the R.A.F. team that flew to Lisbon to play the Portuguese Army team on 17th February, 1946. The Air Force team assembled in London on the Thursday evening, and we began discussing the future of air travel. Bert Brown took great delight in putting the rumour round that the wife of our trainer, Dick Goffin, had taken a special precaution to check up on Dick's insurance policies. Of course, this wasn't true, but it brought some laughs and wise-cracks from the players.

The party took off in a Dakota from Hendon on Friday morning. Our first landing was at St. Mawgan for refuelling. There were several hundred Portuguese at the airport when we landed at Lisbon, but the pleasant surprise as far as I was concerned was the sight of an airport waiter bringing us a basket of oranges and bananas. They were the first bananas I had seen for nearly six years. The only member of the party not really appreciative of this Lisbon luxury was Laurie Scott of the Arsenal, now managing Crystal Palace, who is not a good " sailor " in the air.

We stayed at beautiful Estoril, often referred to as the playground of Europe. I was impressed by this gay spot lying some eight miles from Lisbon, with palm trees running into the drives. I never knew there were as many reporters or photographers in the world as visited us at our hotel. They came by day and night. It was almost impossible to take a walk without a flash-light " exploding."

After dinner we went to the Casino, some fifty yards from our headquarters. Stan Mercer, of Leicester, who was my room-mate for this trip, Neil Franklin, Bert Brown, George Patterson and myself tried our luck at roulette. Need I add, without success!

Wherever we went we saw bananas, and Laurie Scott, now recovered from the effects of the flight, too advantage of this special privilege. In the hotel the porter took it as a great honour to bring us the fruit we had not seen in England for so long. The best laugh was provided by Harold Hobbis of Charlton, who came along as reserve; he chipped in to boast he was a linguist, and as if to prove this statement, called to the porter: " Charlie, old boy, how about a banana? " The porter did not turn his head.

Naturally we pulled Harold's leg, but he was not to be outdone so easily as that. " All you have to do," he explained, like a teacher trying to make a lesson easy for a class of children, " is to add ' io ' on to any English word, and the Portuguese understand you like this."

With that Hobbis shouted out: " I say, Charlio! " Believe it or not the porter turned round with a smile almost as big as himself spread across his face. Harold stuck out his chest at his achievement: " What did I tell you, chaps? " he chuckled, " I speak any language, including Englishio! "

Everybody in Lisbon wanted to see the game, and Portugal, like any other country, has its fair share of ticket scalpers who demanded, and received, £15 for tickets that provided a seat on marble slabs. Wherever we went crowds stood in the streets and gazed at us as though we were from another world.

Nearly 60,000 had packed into the National Stadium by the time we trotted out for the match on Sunday afternoon. While we were engaged in our usual pre-match spot of practice there was a terrific roar when the Portuguese players ran on to the field wearing their military caps. The national anthem of Portugal was played. We stood to attention, and the Portuguese players gave a salute.

It is interesting to note that they saluted in the manner an English troop salutes an officer, and did not give the Fascist salute as was expected. This killed rumours that the Portuguese were going to ask the R.A.F. team to give their national salute.

Lisbon had been politically tense that week-end, and it had been whispered to one or two of us that anti-government demonstrations could be expected at the match. Precautions were taken by the Portuguese police who gathered in strong force round the stadium. There were not any political demonstrations, but the police were needed when thousands of disappointed fans rushed the gates to get in, and were sent back by half-a-dozen police who charged with swords drawn.

The game was played in dazzling sunshine, watched by spectators in brightly coloured shirts, and if it did not come up to the standard of a first-class English game it was enjoyed by the crowd—particularly as the R.A.F. team, which fans insisted on labelling as "England," was held to a draw. Portugal scored first after thirty minutes when their 21-year-old outside-left, Rogerio, who was easily their best footballer, and one of the fastest wingers I have seen, chipped a lovely ball into the goal-mouth for Peyroteo, the Portuguese centre-forward, to nod past Bert Williams, the Wolverhampton goalkeeper. It was a shock for us, but we fought back and five minutes later were on terms when Leslie Smith (Aston Villa) cracked in one of his best drives. You could have heard a pin drop for a couple of seconds after the goal had been scored, so shocked were the crowd, but as soon as they recovered they gave us a fine cheer.

There were not any further goals, and the crowd at times showed their disapproval of the decisions of Dr. Lasalle, the French referee, by whistling. This was somewhat of an injustice to the efficient doctor because the Portuguese were completely puzzled by the off-side tactics of Laurie Scott, Neil Franklin and Geoff Barker.

The crowd thought their national team was getting something of a raw deal from Dr. Lasalle, and they did not spare him with their barracking when the final whistle blew, and he walked off the field.

I heard afterwards that British Soccer prestige slumped in Portugal because we could only draw 1—1. I do not accept this as being the true reaction of the Portuguese, because they were the first to appreciate we were playing under a handicap, having flown from England. Add to this the fact that a smaller ball than we play with in England was used, and I think the R.A.F. eleven did well to draw against a team that would give trouble to some of the best League clubs in this country. And, in any case, English football prestige was more than restored when, on my return to Lisbon in the England team, we defeated Portugal 10—0 in the same National Stadium in May, 1947.

In Lisbon I was nick-named Mateus. They had a wing-half of this name, and at the banquet after the match I was introduced to him, and Hobbis insisted he must be my long lost brother. For some days after the trip the boys took great delight in calling me Mateus.

Sometimes on my travels on foreign soil I am cheered by the unexpected sound of an Englishman—or better still, a North Staffordshire tongue. It happened after this game. We were in the bus being driven back to Estoril, and I was remarking to Frankie Soo at the amazing number of cars on the road, adding that there obviously was not a petrol shortage in Portugal, when one of the cars came alongside us and did not make any attempt to go ahead. Instead, the driver pulled his window down and shouted out: "We are from Stoke."

Franklin, Soo and I looked at each other in some amazement, and the driver shouted again: "My name's Brown, and I'm from Fenton." He kept alongside until our bus forked right for our hotel. "See you to-night at the banquet!" he shouted as he took the road straight ahead.

We met him that night with his wife and a friend, and learned he was in the pottery business, and had left Stoke many years ago to act as an agent for the business in Lisbon. I found the people of Portugal most hospitable and kind. For instance, they examined our passports with the purpose of finding out if any of us had a birthday to celebrate in our few days' stay in Lisbon. Dick Goffin, the trainer was the lucky one, and he received a bottle of port. I don't think that sort of thing would happen in a hotel back home.

CHAPTER XV

MY BEST GAME—AND MY WORST

"Hat-trick" against the Czechs. . . . On starving and being starved. . . . Willie Hall's triumph. . . . I score for England after five years. . . . Maurice Reeday—the back I could not beat.

WHAT was my greatest game? I have never made up my mind whether it was against Ireland at Old Trafford, Manchester, on 16th November, 1938, when England won 7—0, or when we beat Czechoslovakia 5—4 at Tottenham on 1st December, 1937. Against the Czechs I scored a "hat-trick," and had a generous Press. Against Ireland I claimed only one goal myself, but had the pleasure of helping that great little inside-right, Willie Hall of the 'Spurs, to score five times—in succession too—and so set up a record for England in a full international. Obviously, the rout of Ireland at Manchester was Willie Hall's match, but I also claim it as one of my best matches—if not my best.

It was certainly my happiest match, because a week earlier Hall had been my partner at Wolverhampton in the Football League team against the Scottish League, and I had been severely criticized for starving Hall. In fact, one critic had put up this heading in large type: "Matthews starves Hall out of England team." You can imagine how sick I felt when I read this. Willie has always been a good friend to me, and if I had been guilty of rendering him disservice it was unintentional. The thought that Hall might lose a "cap" against Ireland through my fault was the source of much misery to me. When the team to meet Ireland was announced I could have danced round the room when I read Hall had been chosen as my partner.

Whatever mistakes I had made at Wolverhampton would be put right now. I was grateful to the selectors for giving me the opportunity. It is interesting to point out that Willie was as surprised as I at the Press allegations and certainly did not bear me any ill-feeling. The fact that he suggested that we should be room-mates on the eve of our date with Ireland surely killed the rumours I had deliberately given him the frozen-mitt a week before. What really had happened was that the ball had run kindly for me, and I found I could beat the Scottish League left-back, and become a danger-man.

Oddly enough, five years later when England beat Wales 8—3 in a war-time international at Wembley on 25th September, 1943, the sporting press accused the rest of the England team of deliberately starving me out of the game. Just as Willie Hall was not aware of the "freeze out" so also was I oblivious of the fact that I was being deliberately shut out. I did not feel annoyed with my colleagues, and put the "starving" down to the fact that the ball ran the other way. England won 8—3, and that was all that mattered. That was the comment I made to the football reporters who rushed to interview me after the game. I think they had expected to find an indignant Matthews that day.

Stan Cullis told the reporters it was all part of a plan to fool the Welsh defenders. Said the England captain: "Ted Robbins, the Welsh F.A. Secretary, had been planning for days how Wales should stop Matthews. So I decided on a counter-plan. Hughes, the Welsh left-back, and Burgess, the left-half, were watching Stan all the time. This gave Carter, Welsh and Hagan plenty of room in which to move, and the result was the Welsh half-back line was so busy checking this trio that they were able to devote little time to helping their own forwards." Controversy ranged in the Press for days. The stories and rumours became so great that the Football Association issued a statement that letters had been received from some of the England players deprecating suggestions that there was even the slightest jealousy of Matthews or any attempt to ostracize him on the field.

Stan Cullis had let himself in for it, but let me make it clear right now that if Stan had made any pre-match plan to starve me that day he certainly did not confide his secret to me. Cullis was one of the best skippers I have ever played under. He gave the whole team a superiority complex before we went on the field. It was almost as good as starting the game with a goal in hand, and whatever tactics he chose were O.K. by me.

I have wandered a little from the Willie Hall triumph at Manchester five years earlier, but I considered it most important to give these two examples of how it can appear that a player is being deliberately starved without even the players themselves knowing much about it.

Although Hall and I were room-mates, we did not discuss the incident nor did we even suggest one single move or tactic to be used against Ireland's defence next day. Yet as the game worked out it must have appeared to the onlookers that Bill and I had sat up half the night planning the downfall of Ireland and the beating of Billy Cook, the Irish and Everton left-back. Everything went well for Hall and myself that day. The dapper Cook did everything he knew to stop us, but failed, and I recall him remarking to me half-way through the second half: " Stan, if you bring that ball near me once more I'll wring your neck, so help me I will."

I can understand how Billy Cook must have felt because the understanding between Hall and myself in the first half had been uncanny. Willie knew just when to slip outside or to run forward or when to stand still. He never put a foot wrong.

Besides claiming an England scoring record Willie must have also registered the fastest hat-trick in international football. He scored three goals in three and a half minutes. In view of the criticism against me the previous week it was comforting to know I had supplied four of the passes that went towards Hall's five goals. I scored the seventh England goal, seven minutes from time, when the Irish defence was demoralized and at a standstill, and I was able to run half the length of the field, and end up by slipping the ball into a small space between the far post and Twomey, Leeds United's goal-keeper.

Funny that although this was Hall's greatest triumph I should get so much of the cheering. Willie Hall was one of the finest inside-rights of all time. His style of play was so unassuming—just like Willie himself—that his greatness was not always appreciated. He was one of the best partners I ever had.

It was tough blow to him when he lost his right foot early in 1946 as a result of thrombosis, and has since had to undergo a further amputation on his left leg, but I am glad to see Willie is still taking a keen interest in the game. When I saw him some months after the amputation had taken place, he was leaning on crutches, and I asked him how he was getting on. "Fine, Stan," he replied. "Only trouble is that whenever I see a stone or brick in a street I go to kick at it, and find myself doing a thing I never used to do—kicking over the top of the ball." Willie laughed as he said it, and although I felt a pang for the great little 'Spur I also felt proud to have known, and to have played with, such a courageous footballer as Hall.

In spite of the day when the ball ran well for me at Manchester, I know some of my supporters will regard my "hat-trick" against Czechoslovakia as my best performance. I had a good match that day at Tottenham, and played the most important part of the game at inside-right, following injuries to George Mills, the Chelsea centre-forward, and Jack Crayston, the Arsenal right-half, who each took turns at outside-right.

The Czechs were a fine side—one of the best Continental sides I have ever played against. After we had gained a 3—2 half-time lead the Czechs fought back so well, that they were level at 4—4 with only a few minutes remaining. The game was finished almost in darkness. We had taken it for granted the match would now end in a draw when I came into possession of the ball near the half-way line. I took it down, zig-zagged through the darkness into the goal area. Then I fired. Planicka, wonderful Czech goalkeeper, probably would not have seen the shot anyway in the bad light, but when the ball glanced off the shoulder of right-back Kostalek, he did not have the slightest chance. The goal was credited to me, and gave me my first and only hat-trick in international football. Strangely, all three goals were shot with my left foot.

To-day nobody could call me a goal-scoring winger. In fact, if ever I get a goal now it becomes "news," a point which I offer in my defence to the charges sometimes made that I am a selfish player. When I ran three-quarters of the length of the field at Manchester to score England's eighth goal against Scotland on October 16, 1943, it was the first goal I had scored in an international for five years.

Incidentally, this 8—0 win was the biggest ever recorded since the England-Scotland games began in 1872, although war-time internationals will not count as full internationals. Oddly enough, this game against Scotland was played less than a month after the match against Wales, when it had been suggested I had been deliberately starved. In the Manchester game every member of the England team seemed to provide me with passes—no doubt they were out to prove that the way the ball went in the Welsh match was entirely coincidence—just as I felt about Willie Hall when the same charge was made against me.

I have never had a serious quarrel with the Press. I hope I never shall. The football writers can make and break a player. The supporters are swayed by the newspapers. Throughout my long career I have had more good breaks than bad ones from my many newspaper friends. They are too many to name in person, but they are all good fellows.

I have told you about my best games. What about my worst? There was, of course, the game against Switzerland at Zürich in 1938, when Lehmann, the swiss left-back, and dance-band leader, played me out of the game to such an extent that I might just have well yodelled and listened for the echo from the mountains. Neither am I forgetting my match against Germany at Tottenham in 1935. But I would say my three worst games were played a couple of seasons before the war against a Leicester City left-back named Maurice Reeday. He was the most difficult back I ever opposed. It began when Stoke City were drawn to meet Leicester City in the Cup, and by chance we were due to play the same club in a League match at Stoke the Saturday before the cup-tie. Quite honestly, I had not even heard of Reeday up to that League game. In fact, I did not know his name until after the game, when I grabbed a programme, anxious to find the name of my tormentor. I had begun by playing him in the same fashion that had taken me along nicely against defenders with big reputations. I did not get hot under the collar when I found my early attempts to run round him failed, but I did get concerned when I discovered that the longer the game lasted the easier he found it to rob me of the ball.

Change of tactics on my part was obviously required, so I moved to inside-right. Yet I lost the ball the first time it came to me. I went inside-left. Mister Reeday was there again to take the ball off me. Eventually, fed up with my failure, I said: "Haven't you a home to go to?" He grinned and replied: "Yes, but it wont blow away until the game's finished."

When the game was over I began working out plans how to beat Reeday, and I spent some anxious hours during the next seven days. And so to the cup-tie. I could do nothing. Reeday completely blotted me out of the game, although Stoke managed to draw 2—2. I dreaded a third meeting. The replay went the same way. I could not do a thing right against Reeday. I have often wondered why more was not heard of him. The last I heard of him was that he was working in a factory.

CHAPTER XVI

WE SLAM THE NAZIS

I miss the Führer. . . . I take stock of Muenzenberg.. . . . Willingham looks after "Saucepan". . . . We give the Nazi salute. . . . Göbbels, Göring, Hess and a half-dozen Union Jacks. . . . The Swiss put it across us. . . . I fall for the leader of the band.

VICTORY is always sweet, but the sweetest victory I ever tasted was when we licked the Nazis 6—3 in Berlin, on May 14, 1938. This gave me more satisfaction than the defeat of the Italian team at Highbury. The memory I shall always carry of the day we won a victory on Hitler's front door-step is of a tall distinguished-looking gentleman stepping into the England dressing-room after the game, and saying almost casually: "Well played! You have done a good job for England this afternoon."

I felt proud as did the rest of the team, for the bearer of such praise was the late Sir Nevile Henderson, who was at that time British Ambassador to Berlin.

This match was played at a time when Europe was in a state of jitters. Hitler had been making his fanatical speeches at regular intervals. Small countries were being bullied and threatened as the German Führer boasted of the destiny of Germany for the next thousand years. To make matters worse, Hitler's stooge, Mussolini, had been posing on his Rome balcony, and drunk with the success of his partner in crime, was warning the troubled world that whatever happened, Italy would march alongside Germany. The fate of Czechoslovakia was about to be decided and the word "Sudetenland" was on the tip of every tongue in the world as the dictators of Germany and Italy planned the rape of Czechoslovakia.

I had been "capped" in all the internationals of 1937-38, and was delighted to find I had retained my place for this out-of-season tour. I felt excited, and longed to move about in Germany to get the reaction of the common German towards the coming war, for come it had to. We were a happy party that sailed from Harwich. My colleagues were: Vic Woodley (Chelsea), Bert Sproston (Leeds United), Eddie Hapgood (Arsenal), Ken Willingham (Huddersfield

Town), Alf Young (Huddersfield Town), Don Welsh (Charlton), Jackie Robinson (Sheffield Wednesday), Frank Broome (Aston Villa), Len Goulden (West Ham), and Cliff Bastin (Arsenal). With us as reserves were Stanley Cullis (Wolverhampton Wanderers), George Bateman (Brentford), and Harry Clifton (Chesterfield).

I came eye to eye with my first Nazi on the Dutch-German frontier, and was disappointed by the frightened little official who seemed so anxious to show he was doing all he could to help us. In Berlin, we were given little welcome, apart from a few heel-clicks and salutations by officials who must have been rehearsing for the day when the order was given to them to step into uniform so that they could heil and heel-click to their heart's delight.

We arrived in Berlin two days before the match was due to be played and, not unnaturally, I was curious to get a glimpse of the most hated man in Europe, and with this ambition at the back of my mind I went off on a sight-seeing expedition with Bert Sproston. It almost happened. I was sipping a cup of tea with Bert in a small café when there was a sudden rush to the door. Hungry men left their food to stand spell-bound like statues. Women waved handkerchiefs, and even children stopped playing. All I could see was a crocodile-like procession of motor bikes, S.S. men and a couple of large black limousines.

"Some big cheese," I muttered to Bert, who replied, "Yes. It must have been somebody important, judging by the rumpus."

A tall German, who had left a glass of beer to join us at the door, leaned over to us smiling, and in perfect English whispered: "You under-estimate the importance of the occasion. Our beloved Führer has just passed by." As he whispered the word Führer he stood to attention, with a far-away look in his eye, and I was convinced that the Nazis really regarded Hitler as a god. Previously, I did not believe such fanaticism was possible. I had believed much of it to be the imagination of Hollywood script writers. I am glad I saw for myself.

Throughout my stay in Germany I did not sense the tiniest piece of hostility. In fact, everybody went out of their way to be nice to us. Much of it may have been a deliberate act, but I honestly believe there were thousands of Germans who genuinely liked us. The only complaint I had of the trip was that everybody I met wanted to tell me what a wonderful man Hitler was, and that he was working only for the greatness of Germany and the peace of Europe.

In spite of their friendliness towards us there was not any doubt in any of our minds that the Nazis wanted to win this match more than anything else in the world. Equally certain was the fact that we realized there was more at stake than just a football game. This day as never before would we be playing for England.

Whatever one's opinion of Germans may be, I doubt if many will dispute the thoroughness of their organizing powers. The huge Olympic Stadium in Berlin is one of the finest arenas in which I have played, and the turf was as springy as a diving board. The Nazis had chosen the best footballers in Germany and Austria, and had taken their party off for ten day's concentrated training in the Black Forest. With them went the best food, and the finest physical culture doctors throughout Germany. They discussed plans and counter-plans with such regularity that they should have been able to play together blind-folded. A general could not have prepared for a battle with more care. In fact, it was a battle for which the Nazis were preparing. It was to be a test of the New Order—the strength-through-joy boys against the decadent apostles of democracy.

The England team prepared for the game like any other match. We had just finished a hectic eight and a half months of English League and Cup games. On top of this we had not really recovered from two tiring days' travelling from London to Berlin.

In fact, we must have appeared a pretty washed-up bunch of athletes when we met the Germans on the eve of the game. Perhaps that was the reason why the German footballers and Nazi officials laughed so much that night. Just back from their Black Forest hide-out they were as bronzed as Greek statues. Any one of their players could have been chosen as a model of a perfect specimen of manhood. The English boys were all quiet, but I think I can answer for all the players in declaring we were not worried. This was Germany's hour of triumph. Our time would come on the morrow when the game began, and we had come to Germany to beat them at football—not to parade like supermen.

I gained some satisfaction when I studied Muenzenberg, Germany's left-back, who had blotted me out in my only previous appearance against Germany, on the Spurs' ground three years earlier, and noted he looked much older. It gave me more confidence that I should be able to gain some revenge for my losing duel in London. I also spotted the way in which Ken Willingham was weighing up Szepan (we called him Saucepan), the German inside-left, who had given England so much bother in the Tottenham match.

When we arrived at the wonderful stadium we came in for a surprise on discovering the English dressing-room was situated at the top of a huge stand. There were hundreds of steps to climb to reach the top, and it took us several minutes getting to our room. This may have been all part of the German plan to get us rattled, but the English party that day was a set of pretty even tempered lads, with the result we treated the climb up and down—six times in all—as a great joke. Once we put our feet on to the wonderful turf we knew nothing the Germans could do could worry us.

Only one thing shook us—and shook us badly. Shortly before the kick-off an F.A. official came in to wish us the best of luck. It was then he gave an instruction that caused everyone of us to stop what he was doing and look up with some alarm.

"It has been decided that both teams will line up in front of the distinguished visitors' box," he said. "When our National Anthem is played the German team will salute, so in order to get the crowd friendly towards you we want you to give the Nazi salute during the playing of the German national anthem."

I glanced round the room quickly. Every player had a troubled face. I felt disturbed. What would our friends back home think? Nazism was something that every decent person rebelled against, yet here we were being ordered to hide our true feelings and endorse a political doctrine we detested. I wonder how many of the boys were tossing up with the idea of rebelling against this F.A. order which seemed so weak—the idea of crawling to Hitler and his thugs did not appeal to Englishmen. But the F.A. official pointed out that the international situation was so sensitive at this time that it only needed a spark to set Europe alight. The F.A. had been in close touch with Sir Nevile Henderson and in many ways we ourselves were ambassadors for England that day. It was pointed out that when the British athletic team had given the "eyes right" salute at the Olympic Games in Berlin in 1936 many Germans took it as a deliberate snub. So as much as the boys hated this gesture towards Hitler we agreed to abide by the decision of the F.A. But even to this day I still feel shame whenever I sit by the fire and glance through my scrap book and gaze on that infamous picture of an England football team lining up like a bunch of Nazi robots, giving the dreaded salute.

As we followed Hapgood on to the field the 110,000 Germans gave us generous applause, but it was like a whisper compared with the mad roar that went up when the German team appeared. It was a most impressive sight with the huge stadium dotted with thousands of blazing red swastikas. How brave the half-a-dozen Union Jacks appeared as they waved defiantly in the breeze. Goebbels, Hess and Goering must have enjoyed the scene, carefully planned so that Germany should outshine Britain, and I must confess that up to now England was made to look the underdog. But not for long, and even that thunderous roar from the German crowd did not prevent my hearing a few pipy voices from behind the goal:

"Let 'em have it, England." I later learned the encouragement came from a small band of Englishmen holiday-making in Germany.

If any of the boys who called out to us that day should read this book I want them to know their encouragement really meant a great deal to the England team. We were on our toes from the kick-off, and there just was not any stopping England. In the first few minutes I found Muenzenberg had slowed up beyond even my wildest hope. Add to this the fact that Ken Willingham bottled up "Saucepan" so tightly that the dapper inside-left was not able to engineer one really dangerous move, and you have a pretty good idea why England were leading 4—2 at half-time.

Cliff Bastin, Jackie Robinson, Frankie Broome and I each scored a goal to wreck the extensive plans the Germans had made for a Nazi victory celebration after the match.

We had another example of German thoroughness at half-time. As we walked off a dozen Nazi youth ran towards us with warm blankets to wrap round us on our long trek up the staircase. We appreciated this thought, but not sufficiently to ease up against Germany in the second half when we continued to give the Nazis a football lesson. With Robinson and Goulden adding goals we finished very easy 6—3 winners.

Before the F.A. party left Berlin it was arranged for a German team to visit London in 1940. Perhaps this was Hitler's idea of a joke because the German bombers bombarded Britain's capital without mercy in the autumn and winter of 1940. I really believe the Führer believed he would be in Buckingham Palace within a year or two of that match in Berlin. The Germans took a licking from us in the spring of 1939, but that was nothing compared with the hammering that was to follow. Britain-at-war, like Britain-at-play, is quite a team to beat.

Football is a curious game. From our Berlin triumph we made a thirteen hours' train journey to Zürich where we had a date with Switzerland, and frankly we thought we were on a good thing, because the only previous meeting with the Swiss national team had resulted in a 4—0 win for England at Berne in 1933. We were in for a surprise, because the same team that had beaten Germany 6—3, lost 2—1 to Switzerland, who thoroughly deserved their victory. We were over-confident, but perhaps it was understandable. After all the team was playing well, and there had been thirty hours of continuous rain that had left the pitch of the Hardsturm Stadium in Zürich like a typical English ground in mid-winter. The Swiss football writers declared the pitch would suit England and not the home side. How wrong they were.

Not only the Press, but the Swiss football fans openly forecast we should romp home. I was told I was in for a particularly easy time because Switzerland's left-back—a pleasant fellow by name of Lehmann—was the leader of a popular dance band in a Zürich night-club. He was supposed to stay up till the early hours of the morning, and it was reckoned he would only last for the first half, and after that I would be able to prance round the breathless leader of the band, and give him something to dance about. Never before have I been so grossly misled.

It was Alf Young (Huddersfield Town) who assured me this was true. Perhaps Alf was having his own back for the merciless manner in which we—and I in particular—had teased him in Berlin some days earlier when in putting too much energy into the task of eating a chicken Alf had broken his false teeth. The likeable Huddersfield centre-half was self-conscious and tried to avoid laughing. We did our best to make him open his mouth and reveal the absence of his dentures.

We lined up for the kick-off, but there was not any ball until we heard the drone of an aeroplane above the roar of an excited Swiss crowd. The plane came in, low over the ground, manoeuvred for position, and the pilot dropped the ball right on to the field. We started off happily enough, and when in the first five minutes I was able to trot round Lehmann as I liked, I thought there would be a repetition of the Berlin rout. But soon things did not go so well for England. I realized the band leader could do other things besides wave a baton or blow a trumpet. Whenever I attempted to take the ball down to him he would come in at me like quicksilver and sweep it from my toe. This went on with such monotony that I was hoping and praying he would crack up as the result of the late hours he kept. But there was not a sign of his tiring by half-time. He was galloping about the field like a race-horse, and seemed to have the staying powers of a Marathon runner. At half-time I said to Alf Young: "If that guy really stays up till four o'clock in the morning I suggest we recommend similar training methods for the England team. He's killing me." Alf smiled—his teeth had now been repaired—but that was all, for Young had his own worries trying to hold up Bickel, Switzerland's elusive centre-forward.

The fiery enthusiasts in the red shirts had set the crowd roaring after thirty minutes when Aeby, the left-winger, headed a goal, but almost before the echo of the cheers had come from the mountains, England had equalized from a penalty by Bastin after Jackie Robinson (Sheffield Wednesday) had been brought down.

The score was still 1—1, with twenty minutes to go, when Dr. Bauwens, the German referee, awarded a penalty kick against us

DURING THE TROUBLE AT STOKE IN 1946
The author takes a day off to watch Blackpool play

BLACKEST SATURDAY

Tragic scene a few minutes after the break through of the Bolton disaster

that caused tremendous controversy for weeks afterwards. Young bent forward to meet a centre from the right wing with his chest. The ball bounced a yard in front of him, rose awkwardly on the treacherous surface, and struck his arm. There was, of course, an excited shout of "penalty" from the Swiss players and fans, and cheering when the long-legged and cycle-breeched German referee pointed to the spot. Abegglen, the inside-left and veteran of the side, took the kick and placed it out of Woodley's reach.

We were now up against it, and I could do nothing against Lehmann, who must have been humming the words of "I'll Walk Beside You", so close did he watch me for most of the game. So completely had he taken my measure by the end that he often sprinted over to the other side to lend a hand to Minelli at right-back. If anybody ever tells me I have to oppose a band leader again, I shall go into special training—by staying up all night for a month! I never listened to Lehmann's orchestra, but for my part I must confess this was an occasion when I fell for the leader of the band. We regained some lost prestige when we beat France 4—2, in Paris a week later.

CHAPTER XVII

A BATTLE OF FLOWERS

"Viva Inglese." . . . Willingham's Hula-Hula. . . . Request from Malta. . . . Fighting Joe Mercer to Arsenal's reserve. . . . Piola punches a goal. . . . Crown Prince nearly intervenes.

A YEAR after our triumph in Berlin I was again included in the England party in what proved to be the Football Association's last foreign tour for seven years. Our destination was Italy and the Balkans, and the atmosphere was even more tense and more delicate than it had been on our visit to Germany. Our first match was booked for Milan. Mussolini was breathing war and screaming for Nice, Corsica and Tunis. Backing his ravings were millions of fanatical Fascists who with their cries of "Il Duce," indicated their willingness to march behind their leader and alongside Hitler.

I sigher with some satisfaction when I was chosen, realizing there were millions who would willingly have stepped into my boots. It also meant fresh lands, more sunshine and wonderful scenery. But most of all, I wanted to seen and hear for myself how the Italians and the Balkan people felt towards England during the uneasy spring of 1939. I learned later that the political scene had been so delicate at this time that the F.A. came close to cancelling the tour, following consultation with the British government. In view of our previous experience against the Italians I can realize how worried the F.A. must have been, but as the Milan match worked out, there was little cause for fear.

In fact, the officials, like the players, must have been overwhelmed by the wonderful welcome given us at our first stopping place in Italy—at Stresa where Italian customs officials boarded our train, and we found ourselves in a Battle of Flowers. It might have been a first-night on a Broadway stage. Never before have I seen so many flowers thrown as scores of beautiful Italian girls appeared on the station. They carried their flowers in baskets, wore them in their hair. They whistled, winked and flashed their dark eyes as they kissed the flowers and tossed them into our compartment. They sang and giggled and chattered, and every now and then one of the gorgeous creatures would cry out musically: "Viva Inglese." We were all impressed, and our hearts warmed towards these lovely ambassadresses, and towards the Italian people.

This welcome at Stresa was not an isolated case. At every station where our train halted Italian girls were determined to say it with flowers and I laughed till the tears streamed down my face, when Ken Willingham adorned himself like a South Sea Island beauty and gave a skilled performance of the Hula-Hula for us, and the female audience on the platform. Anyway, the girls enjoyed Ken's effort. In Milan itself the welcome was terrific, and a complete contrast to the cold reception given us in Berlin. I realize, of course, the Italians are more demonstrative and more hysterical than the dour German—or the restrained Englishman. However, it was a nice feeling to see in the spring of 1939, the masses of Italian people going out of their way to show friendship towards Britain.

What followed in 1940 did not bear out their attitude towards us in 1939, but even during the war years, when I sat in my R.A.F. mess, and passed an hour or so thinking back to the day we were fêted in Milan, I could not bring myself to believe the Italian people wanted to fight Britain. Of course, the Milan show could have been one big hoax organized by the Fascists to put us off our guard, but I don't think so. The peasants in a country run by a dictator are but pawns, and the Italian folk who welcomed us so profusely this day must have had heavy hearts when the ill-fated Duce led them into a suicidal war.

As I write these words I have before me a perfect vision of Milan's palatial station—the people of Milan are as proud of this magnificent modern marble construction as they are of the ancient cathedral—

jammed with men, women and children. They sang. They cheered and whistled as they waited for a glimpse of us. If we had been men from Mars I do not think there would have been a bigger turn out. The streets were packed for miles around. Another enormous gathering flocked outside our hotel and sang and chanted for us to make an appearance on the balcony. And finally we made the worried manager of the hotel a happy man by agreeing to step on to the balcony and bowing.

We were a self-conscious bunch as we stood there bowing and waving our hands. The crowd below roared and raised their right arms to give the Fascist salute. There was not any threat in this gesture. They wanted to be our friends. When the fuss died down we returned to the lounge. I was stopped by a small dark man, who asked me in perfect English: "Are you Stanley Matthews?" When I told him he was correct he explained he was one of a large party from Valetta in Malta who had made the journey especially "to see England beat Italy."

Malta did not mean a great deal to me that day, and I did not appreciate how very serious these Maltese were when they implored England to gain an overwhelming victory over Italy.

In the years when Italy tried to bring about our destruction in the Mediterranean, and the people of Malta faced the bombing and blockading by Italy with such valour that the island was awarded the George Cross, my mind went back to the little man from Valetta, who had been so anxious we should hit Italy for six. I am proud to have met some representatives of Malta who have proved they have much of the stubbornness and spirit of the people of Britain.

Milan itself is a wonderful city, and we made a point of spending a day at Como, which stands on the edge of the beautiful lake of the same name. Unfortunately for our sight-seeing hopes, Sunny Italy in May, 1939, was cursed with the weather expected during an English summer, and we had three days of non-stop rain. While we were disgruntled because the torrential rain kept us indoors we did realize the more it rained the more likely was the pitch to suit us on the day of the match, and we were hoping the San Siro Stadium would be like a glue-pot.

The pitch turned out just as we had hoped, but in spite of this we did not enjoy the advantage expected, and the Italians came uncomfortably close to giving us a licking. Long before the final whistle, we were struggling to avoid defeat. When the end came we were relieved to get away with a 2—2 draw. It was just one of those turn-ups one can never account for. By all the rules we should have been too good for the Italians, because we fielded the same team that had gained a great 2—1 win over Scotland at Hampden Park a month earlier, with the exceptions of Frankie Broome (Aston Villa) on the left wing in place of "Pat" Beasley (Huddersfield Town), and George Male (Arsenal), who had been chosen as reserve, but was selected to play in place of Morris (Wolverhampton Wanderers).

Things didn't work out according to the book. Everything began well, with Ken Willingham and Joe Mercer taking complete control of the Italian wings. I found the unorthodox methods of Rava, Italy's left-back, difficult to overcome, but the rest of the English forwards were doing well—that is they were doing well everywhere except in front of goal, where it really mattered. The English exhibition of football must have looked good from the Stadium because the Italians clapped and shouted "Bravo," as we worked the ball along the "carpet" and to and fro like clockwork. It continued like this until near half-time with England easily outplaying Italy but not being able to get a goal. Then suddenly I managed to slip Rava—one of the few times in the game—dribble towards goal and centre for Tommy Lawton's priceless head to nod the ball in.

This made us happy, and I was convinced that having got one goal we should settle down to give Italy a lesson in shooting as well as football, but it was England who was in for unpleasant surprises in the second half. The Italians played like twenty men in the second half. They scrapped their defensive tactics, and from the kick-off tore into us while the crowd, delighted that their sleepy team had shaken off its lethargy, roared approval. We were certainly caught napping by the unexpected burst of energy, and within five minutes Italy had equalized. Bievat, their outside-right, paralysed our defence with a wonderful run almost the length of the field, which he completed by cutting in and leaving Vic Woodley without the slightest chance of saving.

We never recovered from the impudence and brilliance of Biavat's goal, and from this point onwards we were struggling to save a game that had turned entirely in favour of Italy. On the few occasions our forwards did get through to shoot there was always Olivieri—most graceful and daring goalkeeper I have watched—to throw himself spectacularly to the ground, pushing a drive round the post, or springing into the air to punch a ball back into play. Two great drives by Tommy Lawton, a high shot by Frankie Broome, and a ball that had been packed with dynamite when Willie Hall shot were all kept out by the astonishing Signor Olivieri.

As the game progressed it became more and more obvious we could do little against the fury of the Italians, who were getting "stuck in," with sliding tackles.

Fortunately for England, there is always somebody at hand to pull us together when we are rattled by the methods to which we are not accustomed back home. This time it was Joe Mercer of Everton who acted as the fairy god-mother to England. Our defence was unmistakeably rattled by the Italian onslaught, and the attack was showing signs of despair, but Joe, playing the game of his life, tackled the Italians with uncanny speed, and continually pushed the ball forward to an England player. Without Joe that day I think England would have finished second best, because in the worst twenty minutes I have ever experienced in an international game only Mercer seemed to have a grip on things, and by sheer determination and rallying powers he pulled us through.

It was the same fighting spirit of Joe's that played such a big part in Arsenal's revival at the end of the war. Highbury's great pre-war team had grown old together. Stars like Eddie Hapgood, George Male, Jack Crayston, Cliff Bastin had their wonderful careers cut short by the war. Herbie Roberts, the centre-half, died while in the Army. Alf Kirchen, the right-winger, and centre-forward Ted Drake received injuries that put an end to their careers. When Ted was told a back injury meant no more football, he was determined to stay in the game in some capacity, and became the successful manager of Reading.

So successful, in fact, that when Billy Birrell and Chelsea parted towards the end of the 1951–52 season, Ted Drake was the man chosen for the task of improving the disappointing Chelsea team.

With the war over, not only were Arsenal stripped of their old stars, but hostilities had caught out Highbury financially, and with the club in debt to the Prudential Assurance by a figure rumoured to be more than £150,000 it was obvious that George Allinson, then manager, could not sign any fantastic cheques to re-build the side. With Arsenal struggling among the last six or seven clubs in the First Division there was much newspaper controversy at the time declaring "the old Bank of England team," as Arsenal were once called, to be bankrupt.

It was around this time Arsenal secured Joe Mercer's signature from Everton—and at a bargain price around £6,000 or £7,000. Joe at this time was considering retiring. When Arsenal asked him to play for them he said he would be glad to for a season or two, because he felt it a great honour to finish his career with such a famous club.

Joe has never regretted his decision. Since the end of the war he has helped Arsenal to finish top of the League and to win the F.A. Cup. He has been a great skipper, and an example to the younger players who are to follow in his footsteps. Footballers don't come much better than Joe Mercer.

But back to Milan. When England recovered from this bad patch, Italy took the lead with the most clear-cut case of "hands" I can recall. Piola, Italy's centre-forward, came charging into the England goal head first, like a wild bull from the pampas. His target was the ball that came twisting in from the right-wing. George Male hurried in to beat the Italian centre-forward to the ball. Piola slipped slightly, but as he was falling he showed ingenious speed by cracking the ball into the net with a straight right punch that might even have brought an approving nod from Joe Louis. The punch certainly did not have the approval of the England team or of George Male. Piola's wonder punch followed through, and might have travelled several more inches had it not been blocked by George's eye.

Poor George Male. We were sorry for him, but some of our sympathy was delayed because we were so astonished that the quickness of the hand had deceived the eye of Doctor Bauwens, the referee. We had not even bothered to protest, so obvious was the foul, but as we stood waiting for the German official to award a free kick to England, we were flabbergasted as he turned dramatically to the centre of the field and pointed, indicating Italy had scored. How Piola and his colleagues must have chuckled, and how the Italian spectators behind the goal must have gasped. The England players did not see the joke. In one body we descended on Doctor Bauwens to make what we considered a justified protest. The referee ran across to consult a linesman, but to our disgust returned sticking to his original decision.

This was terrible. Here we were fighting for English prestige, and we were being licked—and by a goal that had been punched into the net. Perhaps on second thoughts it was the best thing that could have happened. For while the Italian crowd and team became delirious, we passed the word round that England must not and would not lose. Our dignity had been hurt, and our sense of justice injured, and when Englishmen feel this way look out for trouble. Eddie Hapgood clapped his hands together, a Hapgoodism that interpreted into words meant "get cracking." We certainly responded as the spirit spread through the English team with the speed of a forest fire. Mercer came up with the forwards. So did Willingham, and with the help of some good shoulder-charging we had Italy worried.

I can still see that great centre-half-back, Stan Cullis, his chin jutting out at a dangerous angle, coming through to make it an eight-man England forward line. The Italians wilted before our blitzkrieg.

Five minutes remained, and although we were now on top the

score said we were still one down. Then Willingham came through juggling the ball like the master he was. I called to him, and in a flash the ball came along the carpet to my toes. Away I went until I heard a cockney voice call "O.K., Stan," and I knew Len Goulden had slipped across. I passed, and Len shot. The ball struck Rava, and rebounded to where dapper Willie Hall was waiting. Willie cracked the ball goalwards, and the bewildered Oliveri dived seconds too late. It was a body blow to Italy and the goal was received in silence. But to the England team it was all very wonderful. We had pulled out of the fire a game that seemed all over as far as we were concerned. At least we had not let down the folks back home.

We were not without casualties. My hip-bone was chipped. Willie Hall was limping, and, of course, George Male had a black eye that made him the target of the wise-crackers at the banquet given after the game. Many of the Italian officials sympathized with us over that Piola goal.

I was told the Crown Prince of Italy felt so incensed and embarrassed at the gross miscarriage of justice that he expressed his willingness to consult the German referee immediately, and have the decision reversed. I believe he was dissuaded from this action by Mr. Rous, who is unmatched for his tact on such delicate occasions as these. Our Football Association secretary explained that in sport the decision of the referee must be accepted even though the official should make a blunder. It is this sporting spirit that explains why an England football team is welcome in any part of the world to-day.

CHAPTER XVIII

BELGRADE TURNS OUT AT DAWN

Food shortage and banquets. . . . " Charlie " adopts us. . . . He puts over some " impropaganda." . . . Hapgood and I as passengers. . . . Rumanians greet us with " Loch Lomond " . . . Cockney in King Carol's Palace. . . . No place like home.

WHEN we left Milan for Venice en route for Yugoslavia the people of Milan gave us a regal send-off that was every bit up to the standard of the welcome given us on our arrival. It was good to know a handful of professional footballers were doing what the politicians were failing to accomplish—achieving goodwill between nations.

In fact, wherever the England football team stopped we found nothing but friendliness, and when our party—many of the boys, including myself, were limping—arrived in Belgrade at 6.30 in the morning we were astonished to see a tremendous crowd waiting on the platform. We learned after that those at the head of the crowd took up their places before dawn. The friendliness and warm-hearted welcome of the people of Yugoslavia was, I think, summed up perfectly by the official who began his speech thus: " This is an important and proud day for Yugoslavia. Your visit cements the friendship of our two countries."

The hospitality given us in Belgrade was overwhelming and embarrassing. Although the war was still four months away the country was undergoing a food shortage. The shops were meagrely filled, and private homes could offer little variety and only small quantities. Yet wherever we went there was plenty of food. Banquets were held with elastic courses on the menus. At last my curiosity overcame me, and I asked openly how it was we could be served such extravagant meals while the Slavs went short. I was told Yugoslavia had considered the visit of the England team to be of such importance that orders had been given that nothing should be spared to make our visit a happy one.

The Slavs fêted us wherever we went, and we were closely followed by a van with a leading radio commentator to give an eye-witness account of our movements. If I visited a public building or a cinema it was reported in the newspapers. It was while we were viewing some of Belgrade's picturesque buildings that we came upon " Charlie "—or perhaps I should say " Charlie " came upon us. He was a queer little guy, who apparently knew Belgrade inside out, and who had a profound knowledge of football.

We never employed " Charlie." We never thanked him and we never made a request to him, yet we could not move many yards from our hotel without finding the little fellow close on our heels. Actually, we were at times most grateful for his powers as a courier, because he knew every nook and back-street of the capital, and would rattle off in pretty good English some amazing stories. Every dive, every mountain, every lake, every paving-stone had a legend attached to it, and although we soon began to suspect that our faithful guide was an expert at the art of story-telling he never ceased to hold our interest.

It was when he got on the subject of football in Yugoslavia that we really began to prick up our ears. The Slavs were an unknown quantity at football as far as we were concerned, and " Charlie " talked freely. " It will be murder," he chuckled. " Not one of our boys really knows how to kick a ball." We imagined, of course, that this was an exaggeration, but " Charlie " did make us feel easier after our hectic struggle with Italy. Once he assured me that England would win by at least eight or nine goals because the Slavs were slow on the tackle, and that England would be able to settle down and treat the game as an exhibition. On the eve of the match he bowed his farewell gracefully, and gave a farewell speech with the solemnity of a judge pronouncing the death-sentence. " Gentlemen," he began, " it is with deep regret as a loyal subject of Yugoslavia that I am forced to confess my countrymen have not even a sporting chance of beating England to-morrow. As footballers we are no more than clowns."

Those of us who heard him began to believe he was talking the truth. Perhaps we had come under the spell of this fluent story-teller, who had made my blood curdle only the day before when he related the story of how King Alexander of Yugoslavia had been assassinated when driving through the streets of Marseilles some six or seven years earlier. He told how the boy King Peter had his English education cut short with the call to return to Belgrade to rule an indignant nation shocked by the assassination of its king.

Yugoslavia has gone through much tragedy since those happy days. The German Army swept across the borders violating yet another innocent and peaceful country. And to-day the carefree Slavs I met are under Communist control. Marshal Tito, who rules the country with an iron fist, is at least unique in the sense he is the first " Red Dictator " to defy Moscow.

We had been to Oplenae, where the beautiful church had been built as a memorial to the martyred king, and " Charlie " made past events come to life with such reality that we were beginning to look upon him as something of a genius. But not even his wonderful stories will save him from my tongue if ever I should meet him again. I missed him after the match, but when I limped off with a weary England team, beaten 2—1, by a fast-tackling, fiery set of patriots, I realized that we had been taken for a ride by little " Charlie," who, no doubt, was in some dark alley chuckling at his own queer humour. The old villain must have known the Yugoslav team was one of the best in Europe.

A few words about the game. I spent the day before the match testing my damaged hip. I sprinted, twisted and turned without getting any pain, and so I told Tom Whittaker, who was then the England trainer, I was fit. Tom took my word for it, and the same eleven that drew with Italy was put on the field. But my luck was out for although I spent an hour the previous day giving my injured hip a thorough test it went in the first five minutes, on the first occasion I had to touch the ball. I skipped it beyond Dubac, the Yugoslav left-back, and attempted to sprint past him, but my leg just did not respond and felt as heavy as a wooden limb. I was virtually a passenger from this point onwards. I was not in any great pain, but my leg was stiff, and Dubac could afford to spend some of his time going over the other side of the field to help his right-back. I was most unhappy, because I felt that having told Tom Whittaker I was fit, I had let the side down, but as Tom will vouch, the injured hip had stood up to a pummelling during the test. These things are all in the luck of the game.

I do not wish to make any excuses for this defeat, because the Slavs were such a good team, but I must say in fairness to England that the ball did not run kindly, and with Eddie Hapgood tearing a ligament in his ankle and finishing on the left wing it meant England were without wingers. The important thing, of course, is that Yugoslavia won, and when they scored after fifteen minutes I thought the crowd would never stop cheering. It seemed to last for five minutes afterwards. Soon after half-time Broome gave us a fighting chance with a great first-time goal, but we were having difficulty in holding these Soccer enthusiasts, and Perlic, the outside-left, scored the goal that meant our defeat.

It was a truly wonderful feat on the part of Yugoslavia, but coming on top of the not too successful display against Italy we were not a particularly optimistic or happy party that set off for Bucharest next day for our third and last match of the tour—against Rumania. I shall never think of Bucharest without humming the haunting "Blue Danube"—and I shall always end up by laughing. It had been arranged we should make the trip from Belgrade to Bucharest by river steamer to give us the special treat of sailing down the Danube that Strauss made us believe to be so blue. We were nearly fourteen hours on the river, and never before have I seen so much brown water being churned up—not even from the Trent, as it passes through Stoke.

All I can think of is that Strauss was wearing coloured glasses when he was inspired to compose his great work. Or perhaps Strauss saw beautiful things that professional footballers would not appreciate. I don't suppose the Viennese master, were he alive to-day, would get a kick out of the Hampden Roar or from watching a forward scoring a goal from thirty or forty yards out. So believing everybody should stick to their own trade, I will not dispute that the Danube was blue when Strauss wrote the waltz that is known throughout the world.

As in Italy and Yugoslavia the welcome given us by the natives was astonishing. When we disembarked at Turnu-Severin at 7.30 in the morning, we were not only greeted by sprays of flowers and flags, but by the town band which puffed out "John Peel," and as many other British tunes that could be crammed into the short time we were there.

The tune that got the biggest laugh from the boys was "Loch Lomond," played at a speed that left the willing Rumanian musicians breathless. Surely, the only time in history an English party has been greeted by a Scottish tune in Rumania!

In Bucharest there was more band-playing, more speeches, more flags and more flowers. Wherever we went we were followed as though we were super-men, and our defeat at the hands of Yugoslavia did not appear to make us any less important in the eyes of the Rumanians. The most fascinating part of our stay in Rumania, as far as I was concerned, was the visit to the oilfields at Ploesti, which surely had a just claim among the wonders of the world—until R.A.F. and American bombers visited it during the war and smashed Hitler's life-line to smithereens.

If only the proud Rumanian officials who showed us their masterpiece of engineering could have known that a few years later the R.A.F. would be shattering the mighty derricks and wells it would not have been flowers that they would have been showering on us!

Ploesti is a wonderful place. Those of you who saw a film shown four or five years ago with the title of "Boom Town," will have some idea of what it is like. That film showed a miniature Ploesti—a great forest of towering derricks. What a tragedy for Rumania and for her "Boom Town," that she was dragged into the war by Hitler. The R.A.F. Liberators did such a thorough job that Ploesti was damaged beyond repair as far as Germany was concerned.

Fresh derricks have been built, and the oil is gushing as freely as ever, but Rumania, like Yugoslavia, has come under the domination of the Communists. The Balkans has always been a hot-bed of intrigue and strife, and to-day we consider Rumania as rather sinister because we know little about anything happening behind the "Iron Curtain." But I can only talk about Rumania and the Rumanians as I knew them in the spring of 1939, and I look back with happy memories because they were a friendly, light-hearted people.

While sight-seeing we naturally looked in at Pelash Castle, the magnificent home of King Carol and Madame Lupescu. Until I had seen it I had never believed such dream palaces or fairy castles as are sometimes illustrated in Hans Anderson fairy-story books really existed. Pelash Castle was almost too wonderful to be real.

But it was while we strolled round open-mouthed and somewhat dazed that we were brought quickly to reality by a shrill Cockney voice grumbling: "Cor, lumme, that ain't the wye to prune roses. Gimme the scissors." Fantastic if you like. Here we were strolling round the fairy-palace of a real king hundreds of miles from England, and we hear a voice of somebody obviously born within the sound of Bow Bells! The speaker was delighted to meet us, and explained he was from the East End of London, and had a good job on King Carol's household staff. We took the opportunity of making a few cracks at the expense of Len Goulden, declaring the Cockneys even ruined the beauty of a fairy palace, but Len—himself an East-End boy—was quick to come back with the boast that there was usually a Cockney in the England team.

On the day of the match I was an onlooker, as it had been discovered I had chipped my hip-bone. Hapgood, Willingham and Willie Hall joined me in the stand. Frank Broome took my place on the right wing, and Leslie Smith, who was then with Brentford but is now with Aston Villa, received his first "cap," being brought in at outside-left. Goulden went to inside-right and Don Welsh, the merry Charlton forward, now managing Liverpool F.C., came in as inside-left. Morris (Wolves) took Hapgood's place. Wilf Copping was at left-half, with Joe Mercer crossing over to the right.

England badly needed one win on this tour, and with all these forced changes the English party was a little dubious of our chances, but with Cullis playing at his best, England gained a 2—0 win, thanks to a first-half goal by Goulden and a second-half winner by Welsh.

It was not a great performance by England, but it was at least something to send us away with lighter hearts. Three days later we were gazing at those wonderful white cliffs of Dover which meant home for a weary bunch of footballers. When we stepped ashore there were no bands to welcome us; no flowers; no flags. We did not mind. There is no place like home.

CHAPTER XIX

FOREIGN CHALLENGE

Dynamic Dynamos. . . . Bouquets of Friendship. . . . I play for Arsenal—at Blindman's buff. . . . English football as she is played. . . . South American threat. . . . They still know how to waltz in Vienna.

THE most sensational and successful challenge ever made to British Soccer prestige came with the visit of the Russians in November 1945. The men from Moscow flew to Croydon after a week of rumour and counter-rumour, and from the moment they landed till the night they threw a farewell party there was never a dull moment in the football world.

The Russians provided the sport columnists with a story every day. They were a law unto themselves, and provided thrills and shocks. They certainly surprised us, and after their opening game at Stamford Bridge, when they held Chelsea to a 3—3 draw, we soon realized the Russians were good enough for our best League sides.

When the Dynamos arrived they were an unknown quantity, and there was some criticism when Chelsea were chosen as the first opponents.

In many quarters it was considered to be too big a test to expect a Russian team to be up to the standard of a First Division English club. The Dynamos, however, insisted on playing in London against a well-known club, and it was only after much patient explaining by Mr. Rous that they accepted a mid-week fixture.

The Russians argued that Saturday was our big football day, and they took it as an insult to ask them to play in a mid-week fixture. "If a British team played in Moscow," they explained, "all other games would be stopped." The Football Association secretary had to explain that in England he did not have power to disrupt eighty-eight League matches, and that he could assure them there would be a big crowd in mid-week, pointing out that many internationals in England are played during the week.

The Russians must have been pleasantly surprised by the welcome given them on their opening game. I think every office boy in London had a grandmother die that day. Eighty-five thousand packed into Stamford Bridge. Cars started traffic blocks miles from the ground. Ambitious spectators risked their lives climbing girders and over the grandstand. There were one or two minor accidents when spectators crashed through the glass roof on to the crowd below. Before the kick-off thousands of spectators broke on to the pitch, and the police decided it would be safer to let them remain on the touch-lines.

First surprise was when the men from the Soviet Union came out carrying bouquets of flowers. They lined up opposite their opponents, and with dramatic ceremony stepped forward and presented a bunch to each Chelsea player.

It stunned the crowd, who had never seen anything like this before. The Chelsea players appeared a little surprised and embarrassed, but when the crowd realized the full significance of this gesture of friendship there was a terrific roar of approval.

Shocks followed throughout the match. The Russians played at a terrific pace, and demonstrated the important part fitness plays in Soccer. They played some of the most attractive football seen for years, and their ability to pass the ball to one another at great speed was astonishing.

I don't think there was a dribbler in the side. All the time the ball was being pushed along the ground—from back to half-back to inside-forward to winger to centre-forward, and at a speed that left Chelsea gasping. One second Chelsea would have the ball in the Dynamos' goal-area, the next it would be Chelsea who were defending.

All that the Russians seemed to lack in the opening half-hour was shooting ability. Goals were missed one after the other, and when Leonid Soloviev, the left-half, missed a penalty and covered his face with both hands, I really thought the Russians would never score.

Goulden and Williams had given Chelsea a 2—0 lead, but more shocks came in the second-half. Kartsev, Dynamos' brilliant inside-right,crashed in a great goal from thirty-five yards just to show the crowd that the Russians could shoot. Inside five minutes Archangelsky, a late right-wing choice, equalized. The crowd rose to the Russians who had shown true fighting spirit. I traced some sympathy in the shout that went up when Tommy Lawton slipped Semichastny, the Russian captain, to head Chelsea's third goal, nine minutes from time. But once again the Dynamos struck back, and Bobrov equalized. four minutes from time.

The next game was at Cardiff on the following Saturday. The Russians did not like the idea of leaving London or playing a Third Division team, but finally agreed. Cardiff had a good young side, and their manager, Cyril Spiers, thought his club would put up a better show than Chelsea. We were all wrong. The Russians ran riot to beat the Welsh team 10—1, and to prove beyond any doubt that only the best we had was good enough opposition for them.

The men from Moscow sized up the Welsh boys in the first five minutes, and were so superior that most of the time they were able to walk the ball into the net. After gaining a 3—0 half-time lead Dynamos ran riot in the second-half, with the tall Bobrov doing most of the scheming at inside-left, and centre-forward Beskov helping himself to four goals.

After the game the disappointed Mr. Spiers declared the Russians to be the finest football machine he had ever seen. Most of the folk who saw the Cardiff game were of the same opinion.

As I saw it the secret of the Russians' success in England was their wonderful ball control, plus exceptional fitness. I was hoping they would either come to Stoke, or that a match would be arranged against an England XI, so that I might get the opportunity to try my luck against them. It did not look as though my wish would be realized because the next two fixtures arranged were against Arsenal and Glasgow Rangers.

When I heard George Allison was in a jam to raise a strong team my hopes were raised. The Dynamos particularly requested a match against Arsenal, but Mr. Allison pointed out he could not raise a strong team, and sought permission for Leslie Compton, Reg. Lewis and Bernard Joy, on service duty in Germany, to be brought home for the match.

Neil Franklin, the Stoke centre-half now with Hull City, and I asked Bob McGrory to ring Mr. Allison to offer our services. The Arsenal manager was delighted, but pointed out he had had word Bernard Joy would be able to get home from Germany, which meant Neil was not required at centre-half. I was more fortunate as Arsenal were without a right-winger. The queer line-up of the Arsenal team —Frank Butler called it " George Arsenal's XI "—was: W. Griffiths (Cardiff City), Scott, Bacuzzi (Fulham), Bastin, B. Joy, Halton, Matthews (Stoke), Drury, Rooke (Fulham), Mortensen (Blackpool), Cumner.

It was just my luck after having looked forward to this opportunity for days that one of London's thickest pea-soup fogs should come down on the day of the match. It must have been the strangest game that 54,000 fans, who paid £10,000, *never* saw. All they witnessed was a game of blindman's buff.

Nearly everybody agreed the game should never have started. It did—and what is more surprising—it finished, but must go down as the most farcical match on record. Not only did the crowd fail to see any of the seven goals scored—the Russians won 4—3—but I myself could not see more than a yard or so in front of me. The Russians scored in the first minute but Arsenal had established a 3—2 lead at half-time. This was wiped out by another Dynamo second-half rally.

I am afraid the second half is better forgotten. The fog had ruined the game as a spectacle. There was much booing, some fouling, and twice my shirt was pulled out of my shorts, but I have no complaints. A Russian explained afterwards that shirt-pulling is not considered foul tactics in Russia. " After all," he declared, " you can't get a broken leg or bruised knee by somebody pulling out your shirt!"

The Russians played one more match—against the Rangers in Glasgow before nearly 90,000. After a fierce ninety minutes they retained their unbeaten record in Britain, holding the Scottish team 2—2. After this game the Dynamos were called home by Moscow. The news was picked up in England from a Moscow radio station. The Russian party in Britain knew nothing about this, and had been expecting to play an F.A. XI on the Aston Villa ground on the following Wednesday.

In four games more than 260,000 British fans watched the Russians and the consensus of opinion was that Dynamos were the finest team to have visited this island.

British sport has suffered as the result of the war more than any other country. We have lived on strict rations, and players in the services were not able to get the special training afforded the Dynamos.

Before the last war England held complete mastery at Soccer, and practically every country throughout the world, with the possible exception of Russia, was willing to admit we were the football bosses. But to-day, while we are not yet prepared to admit we play second fiddle to any country in the world—remember we are still unbeaten on our own soil by any foreign team—we know the red light is shining, and that we are going to have to look to our laurels if we are to hold off the challenge from Russia, Brazil, Austria, Argentina, Spain, Uruguay, Germany, Italy, and other national teams from South America and from behind Europe's "Iron Curtain."

We had a shock in the World Cup series in South America in 1950, and since then have had narrow squeaks in England against Yugoslavia, France, Argentina and Austria, but, nevertheless, we have kept our envied unbeaten home record intact. Later I will deal fully with our failure in the World Cup in South America, but here I want to say a few words about our close calls with other countries.

The first warning of how the Continent had improved was given me after six years of wartime make-shift football when France played us at Wembley on May 26, 1945. French football had improved, and they had copied many of our moves and tactics. There was truth in the Sunday newspaper headline which stated that France had shown "English football as she is played." We had expected an easy victory, but were surprisingly checked by a spot of real French polish and held to a 2—2 draw.

In the 1945–46 season we beat Belgium 2—0 at Wembley, and Switzerland 4—1 at Stamford Bridge, but lost 2—1 to France in Paris. Our defeat in Paris was disappointing because we seemed to have found our best form when beating the Swiss eight days earlier in London. But things just would not go right in the Paris game, and coming on top of an overwhelming defeat for Great Britain at the hands of France in the Davis Cup, the knock-out of Bruce Woodcock by Tami Mauriello in New York, and the defeat of Freddie Mills in a world light-heavyweight championship fight against Gus Lesnevitch in London, British sport had gone through the blackest eight days of its history.

On top of this, the Swedish team, Norrkoping, visited England and beat English clubs with methods we had taught them. We would have laughed at a suggestion in 1939 that a Swedish club could visit England and defeat teams like Charlton, Newcastle United and Sheffield United.

But the decline and fall of England's Soccer Empire did not come about in spite of all the gloomy forecasts. We defied any foreign team to beat us in England, although we did suffer a great loss of prestige

A MATTHEWS DRIBBLE

A Matthews dribble past Pat Beasley in a Cup tie between Blackpool and Fulham.

AUTOGRAPH HUNTING

Stanley Cullis looks on while Field-Marshal the Viscount Montgomery of Alamein signs

by failing to qualify for the Final series of the World Cup down in Rio in the summer of 1950. England's defeat by the part-time professionals of the United States was the biggest Soccer upset of all time.

CHAPTER XX

FLY AWAY FRANKLIN—COME BACK PAUL

South American threat to British Soccer clubs. . . . Colombia tempts England's captain, Neil Franklin, to break away from Stoke City. . . . Roy Paul and Jack Hedley return to England without signing. . . . Charlie Mitten signs for Santa Fé. . . . I am offered a trip to Colombia, but refuse.

THE biggest threat ever to British Soccer was not of a foreign team beating us, but of the remarkable developments in South America in 1950—the year of the World Cup—when Colombia made tempting offers to some of our best stars, and succeeded with fantastic offers in persuading a few to break away from their clubs.

The first warning of this extraordinary business hit England when Neil Franklin, the Stoke City and England centre-half, and his club colleague, George Mountford, together with their wives and families, flew away to Bogota to sign for the wealthy Santa Fé club. Their plan was one of the best kept secrets in Soccer for neither Stoke City nor England had any idea, and it was a shock to the F.A. selectors when Franklin declined to play for his country against Portugal and Belgium in May, 1950.

There were, of course, all sorts of rumours about what Franklin and the Stoke City right-winger received for playing for Santa Fé. The only reason Colombia could make offers far beyond the reach of other countries was that the professional clubs had broken away from F.I.F.A. This meant they were not bound to honour the transfer system at all. And they couldn't care less what the English and Scottish clubs thought about it.

After Franklin and Mountford had made successful debuts, rumours spread quickly that practically every well-known English player had received offers from some Colombia club. Scotland, Wales and Ireland, as well as Brazil and other South American countries, were explored by representatives of the Colombian pirates and at one time several big English teams began to panic. The Soccer Press in quite a few cases sympathized with the fly-away footballers, pointing out that in the football writers' opinion the Football League system was wrong whereby players were transferred for more than £20,000, yet the salaries of the footballers themselves were comparatively small. All sorts of suggestions were put into the newspapers as an answer to this South American scare. One well-known writer suggested the League should immediately make a promise that in future players would receive a fair percentage of any transfer fee. Of course, none of the suggestions were taken up.

Billy Higgins (Everton) and Bobby Flavell (Hearts) followed the Stoke City pair to Colombia. Then Roy Paul (Swansea Town) and Jack Hedley (Everton) were next on the list, but although Paul and Hedley arrived in Bogota they turned down the offer of the Millionarios F.C., and returned to England without playing or signing. My old Blackpool colleague, Jock Dodds, got himself into a bit of trouble. Jock, then with Lincoln City, made it known he was representing the Millionarios club, and was expelled by the Football League for his part in the negotiations. Jock, although not playing League football any longer, is reinstated.

Charlie Mitten, Manchester United's goal-scoring left-winger, left England to join the Santa Fé club just as a somewhat disillusioned Neil Franklin returned home with his wife. Mitten was reported in some of the papers as having received an offer of a down payment of £5,000 and £2,000 a year salary from the Santa Fé club.

Johnny Aston and Harry Cockburn, both of Manchester United, members of the 1950 F.A. party in Canada, who later joined the England World Cup party in Rio, also received offers, but rejected them. I, too, turned down immediately a feeler that was put to me. Later a definite offer was made in which I didn't have to break away from my club, but could have £400 for six exhibition games in June. The Colombian F.A. wanted me to bring three Blackpool colleagues, Harry Johnston, Stan Mortensen and Eddie Shimwell.

The terms were £50 a game, £10 bonus for a win, £5 for a draw, plus £18 a week spending money. Return air fares and first-class hotel accommodation were guaranteed.

George Mountford and Charlie Mitten were the last of the English players to return home. All those who played in Colombia were fined or suspended or both. Franklin, of course, sacrificed his place in the England team, and Stoke City transferred him to Hull City.

Charlie Mitten was also transferred from Manchester United to Fulham after his suspension had ended.

This Bogota business was only a few months' wonder. One or two of the boys did pretty well out of it financially, but I think all who went there realized that England and English football isn't so bad after all. It was fine while the players and their wives lived like millionaires on first arrival, but after the early glamour of strange lands and more ready cash wore off, they found such snags as trying to understand the language and the temperament of the South Americans. They certainly had not discovered a football Utopia. As I myself have so often remarked when returning from a trip abroad: "There's no place like home!"

CHAPTER XXI

NOT SO RIO GRANDE

I am picked to tour Canada—and to join the World Cup party. . . . I am misquoted as taking up a £50 a week job in Canada. . . . Our Rio players estimated at £250,000. . . . The £3,000,000 stadium. . . . Football amid Guy Fawkes explosions.

FROM the beginning of the 1949–50 season the word "Rio" was on the tongue of every footballer, and on the pen of every football writer. For the first time ever England had entered the World Cup series arranged by F.I.F.A., and Rio de Janeiro was to be the venue. What a glamorous setting, and can you wonder why everybody wanted to get into the party that was to fly to Brazil!

My last appearance for England had been in the team beaten 3—1 by Scotland at Wembley in April 1949, and I had been left out of the internationals in the following 1949–50 season. So when I was chosen for the F.A. party to tour Canada and New York, many folk took it for granted that I would be out of the more important England party bound for Rio; but I was not disappointed, because, after being chosen for Canada, Walter Winterbottom phoned me at Blackpool and asked if I was 100 per cent fit, and if I would be prepared to break off from the Canadian party to join the England players in Rio. I naturally said I would be delighted, and one other member of the Canadian party was also invited to go to Brazil. That was Jim Taylor, the Fulham centre-half.

The F.A. party sailed from Liverpool on the *Empress of Scotland* on May 9, 1950. It consisted of: Hanson (Bolton Wanderers), Mozley (Derby County), Milburn (Chesterfield) Ellerington (Southampton), Johnston (Blackpool), Flewin (Portsmouth), Taylor (Fulham), Russell (Wolverhampton Wanderers), Ward (Derby County), Matthews (Blackpool), Sewell (Notts County), Bowyer (Stoke City), Lofthouse (Bolton Wanderers), Vaughan (Charlton Athletic), Hagan (Sheffield United), Wainwright (Everton), Hancocks (Wolverhampton Wanderers), Medley (Tottenham Hotspur).

Mr. H. H. Hughes (Vice-President of the Football Association) and Mr. Richards of Barnsley F.C. were in charge. Mr. Richards took the place of Mr. A. H. Oakley, Wolverhampton Wanderers director and Vice-President of the Football League, who was not well enough to make the trip. T. Dawson (Grimsby Town), a former Stoke City player, was our trainer.

When we docked at Quebec some reporters came aboard and interviewed me, and immediately began asking questions about salaries, expressing great surprise when we told them what we received. The Canadian journalists pointed out that ice hockey and baseball stars would have refused even to make an appearance for what we were paid for playing.

One reporter asked if I would be interested in taking a job as a coach in Canada for, say, £50 a week. Not wishing to appear ungracious I gave him what I thought to be a non-committal reply, saying that if such a handsome offer were made to me, I would naturally have to think about it, because what League footballer could afford to turn down £50 a week without at least giving some consideration to the proposition?

Imagine my embarrassment on picking up a newspaper next morning and reading in glaring headlines that I was definitely coming to Canada to coach for the salary the reporter had suggested. I came to the conclusion that the Canadian journalist in question was really hard-up for a story, and was not letting a little detail like facts kill his enterprise.

There were not many incidents in this tour of a great country and grand people. It would have been all pleasure apart from the terrific amount of travelling that was involved. Our first match was played at Montreal in great heat, and little Johnny Hancocks was the darling of the crowd, scoring four goals. At Toronto we had pleasant surprises, meeting Gracie Fields and Norman Evans. Norman, who lives at Blackpool, knew Harry Johnston and myself, and he invited the whole party to attend the theatre where he was appearing.

Naturally, we went sight-seeing to Niagara Falls, and this is one spectacle I shall always remember. Another highlight was appearing before Canada's biggest-ever Soccer crowd—32,000—when we met and defeated Manchester United at Toronto.

We were treated royally wherever we went throughout this great Dominion. Enthusiasm among the followers of Association Football is encouraging, but although Canada has many part-time professionals, especially from Scotland, Soccer will never take the place of ice hockey or baseball—just as those two games will never become more popular than football or cricket in Britain.

After the Manchester United match, Jim Taylor and I met up in New York with Harry Cockburn and Jack Aston of Manchester United, who were also booked to join the England party at Rio. Harry and Jack had seen more of New York than Jim and I, so when we found there were only two seats available on the plane, it was mutually agreed Taylor and I should spend another day looking round the city of sky-scrapers.

The rest of the F.A. party had come in from Canada, and we had the opportunity of watching the F.A. XI beat America's World Cup team—the same side that was later to cause a Soccer sensation, beating England at Belo Horizonte.

Our best players were already in Rio. Taylor, Aston, Cockburn and myself were joining up with: Williams (Wolverhampton Wanderers), Ditchburn (Tottenham Hotspur), Ramsey (Tottenham Hotspur), Scott (Arsenal), Eckersley (Blackburn Rovers), Wright (Wolverhampton Wanderers), Hughes (Liverpool), Dickinson (Portsmouth), Watson (Sunderland), Nicholson (Tottenham Hotspur), Milburn (Newcastle United), Mortensen (Blackpool), Bentley (Chelsea), Mannion (Middlesbrough), Finney (Preston North End), Mullen (Wolverhampton Wanderers), Baily (Tottenham Hotspur). With all this talent—estimated at £250,000 by writers—we had reason to be optimistic of at least qualifying for the final series, but that was not to be.

Rio, of course, is a South American jewel, and was every bit as beautiful as I had anticipated from scenes I had seen in various films. The buildings consisted of semi-sky-scrapers with pyramid-shaped mountains as a background. The Copacabana Beach where we stayed was some eight miles along the coast from the city of Rio. This was a beautiful scene by night with the twinkling of lights, and the huge flood-lit figure of Christ, poised on the top of Mount Corcovado, with outstretched hands as though protecting the whole city.

Rio is one of the fastest-moving cities I know. London is slow compared. So is Paris, and even New York taxi-drivers aren't such a boon to undertakers as the drivers down in Rio. There isn't any speed-limit, and I must confess the drivers are among the best in the world in spite of their recklessness. The main highway along the Copacabana Beach is dead straight, and the high-powered American Cadillacs raced along that stretch as though at Brooklands. The road was clear one minute, but in the next few seconds you had to jump for your life!

When I arrived in the middle of June I was astounded to learn Brazil's winter had just started. It was still very hot by English standards, but the sun used to go down by four in the afternoon, and it was quite dark around five-thirty. Yet it was hot enough to lie on the beach and sun-bathe, and although the majority of Brazilians did not bother to bathe, any Englishman would have found the water warm.

Some of our boys were disappointed the Beach was put out of bounds. While some of the locals lazed on the sand we were off to sweat as we trained on the pitch of the Botofogo F.C. Of course, Walter Winterbottom was so right in not allowing us to lie about the beach. The sand was hot enough to cook eggs on, and Walter didn't want our energy sapped.

Bathing would have been out of the question anyway, because of the treacherous currents. Many a strong swimmer has been lost, sucked under the fury of the Atlantic breakers. All along Copacabana lifeguards were posted in case some stranger fancied his strength and stamina against what could be the cruel sea.

I was not unduly troubled by the sun although I was grateful that it was only Brazil's winter—I don't think I could kick a ball during their summer—but I still had my doubts as to how our team would stand up under ninety minutes' cooking if we had to face Brazil, whose players revelled in the sunshine. Also at this stage I was wondering whether the original suggestions of perhaps playing under floodlight might not have suited England better.

When the England team to play Chile on the first Sunday was announced, I was not included. Mr. Arthur Drewry, the only F.A. selector with the party, relied on the same side that had done so well against Belgium in Brussels, namely: Williams (Wolverhampton Wanderers); Ramsey (Tottenham Hotspur), Aston (Manchester United); Wright (Wolverhampton Wanderers), Hughes (Liverpool), Dickinson (Portsmouth); Finney (Preston North End), Mannion (Middlesbrough), Bentley (Chelsea), Mortensen (Blackpool), Mullen (Wolverhampton Wanderers).

We took a first look at the huge arena Brazil had built especially for the World Cup at a cost exceeding £3,000,000. It looked a grand stadium, built in a complete circle with thousands of bright-blue tip-up seats, because Brazilians like to watch their Soccer in comfort. The Brazilians slipped-up on their time-table, however. When they started erecting the stadium in August 1948, they were confident everything would be completed in time for the World Cup nearly two years later. With the first match of the series opening between Brazil and Mexico the next day, there were still 7,000 workmen tearing down the scaffolding to get the stadium tidy. We were informed the seating accommodation was 130,000 with room for 25,000 standing.

From the stand, the grass looked beautiful—almost as perfect as Wembley, but we were in for disappointment when, after inspecting the dressing-rooms, we strolled on to the pitch. It was far from the carpet of Wembley or of the National Stadium at Lisbon. It consisted of local turf, the grass spread out sideways with the blades entwining.

Our first match against Chile was not until Sunday, but we were anxious to get some of this Rio Soccer atmosphere which we had heard so much about, and of course made the journey on the Saturday to the opening match between Brazil and Mexico. I certainly do not remember scenes quite so fantastic.

The traffic jam was worse than we expected although we had been warned to leave for the match early. We left our hotel at Copacabana in good time, but were nearly two hours getting within sight of the ground. Hundreds of cars were abandoned miles from the statium. We, too, had to abandon our coach and push our way, as best as we could, through the huge crowd.

Inside, the scenes were crazier than outside. 80,000 excited Brazilians stood up and screamed with delight when the national side came running on to the pitch. Hundreds of explosives were tossed freely into the air, and for some minutes the sky was black with sulphur and smoke. It really was like one of the blitzes of the last war. Then balloons went up, followed by the releasing of 5,000 pigeons. Before Brazil kicked off there was a salute of twenty-one guns. I tell you, I have never seen anything like it before or since. It was a real Guy Fawkes celebration, and I remember how odd it was to look at that magnificent figure of Christ with the hands stretched out in peace looking on the noisiest football I can recall.

This was my first glimpse of the Brazilian team, and, as I sat in the stand, I thought England was sure to beat them. They were good footballers, mark you, but they didn't get on with the job too well although beating the weak Mexican side 4—0. I could see gaps down the middle, and I had a mental picture of Stan Mortensen galloping through and causing chaos. Frankly, I thought to myself England would win the World Cup if Brazil was regarded as our chief danger. But how wrong I was.

In fact, when I sat in the stand again next day watching England beat Chile 2—0, I was forced to admit our boys had not shown anything like true form, and it was a warning of what was to come.

We had no need to worry about the heat because a storm broke over Rio, and up to a few hours before the kick-off torrential rain fell. So much so that it embarrassed the Brazilians, so proud of their unfinished stadium.

The rain poured through large cracks in the roof, and the blue tip-up seats became soaked. Fortunately, the rain stopped before the kick-off, and the England team was playing under pretty normal English conditions.

In the Chilean team was an old friend. I refer, of course, to George Robledo, the Newcastle United inside-forward. George was born in Chile, although he has spent most of his life in England. His countrymen considered him to be the greatest footballer ever to come out of Chile. George was the only professional in their side. The rest of them consisted of engineers, bootmakers, accountants, and grocers. They get £14 a month to carry on as part-time footballers.

Their goalkeeper and captain was a handsome Spanish-looking chap, named Sergio Livingstone Eves. He was forty years of age, but looked much younger. I asked him the reason for his very English name, and he informed me his grandfather was from England.

England did not shine. We won 2—0, and that was good enough, but while the Brazilians thought we were strolling to an easy win, we were, in fact, struggling. Several of the boys told me after the game they had not found their breathing too easy. Still England had cleared the first hurdle, and now we had to tackle the United States at Belo Horizonte nearly 300 miles away. That should be easy, because hadn't I watched the F.A. beat them in New York just over a week earlier. Little did I expect the blackest mark on England's international record was to come. Yes, the Yanks with their part-time professionals licked us. It was a bitter pill to swallow.

CHAPTER XXII

BEAUTIFUL HORIZON?—SEZ WHO?

Guests at a Gold Mine. . . . The result that shocked the world—England 0, United States 1. . . . Spain, or bust—and we bust. . . . Brazilian crowd wave handkerchiefs to us and chant "Adios".

IT was quite a confident party that flew out from the Santos Dumont airport bound for Belo Horizonte, which interpreted is "beautiful horizon." But we were being kidded, because when we returned with our tails down the city was—for us at any rate—the Lost Horizon!

There remain in Brazil thousands upon thousands of miles of

unexplored territory, and but for the progress of flying, Brazil would be well behind the times, because there are few good roads or railway tracks. I was told it would take fourteen hours for a train to chug through the mountains to Belo, whereas the flying time was around one hour! Belo Horizonte is a modern city of sky-scrapers, and after flying above nothing but mountains, rivers and lakes you suddenly come upon this city whose buildings have sprung up like mushrooms since it was first planned fifty years ago.

We were to be the guests of the St. John d'el Ray Mining Company, a British firm who have been situated in the State of Minas Geraes, for more than 100 years. The owners of the mine put their camp entirely at the disposal of the English players and Press. And what an attractive camp, too, at Morro Velho close to the little town of Nova Lima which was sixteen miles from Belo itself.

What a fantastic drive it was from the airport to the mine along a red-dust road cut out by the mine people with nearly two hundred hair-pin bends. Brazilian drivers, as I said earlier, are wonderful, but so reckless, and I doubt if the driver who escorted us to our headquarters knew how many scared passengers he had behind him. On this scenic road there was a drop each side without curbs. One slight error by the driver would have sent us all crashing into the gaps below. We arrived safely, but our faces and mouths were covered in the red dust which had blown through the window as we sped along. It was good to meet Englishmen and their wives at the camp, and I think they were equally delighted to see us, and talk about things back home.

Certainly, never before have I met such hospitality. The bosses of the mine told us we had only to ask to receive. If we raised a finger, one of the servants would run to ask what was our wish. Iced drinks were brought frequently, and we weren't even allowed to pay for the stamps on the letters we were sending home. If we wanted a car or a mule, we only had to ask, although we preferred to spend our time taking it easy.

The food was cooked in English fashion and was excellent, and although there was little to do in Nova Lima, there was a friendly club-house at the mine, and some of the boys enjoyed snooker, darts or card-games in the evenings.

I was not chosen to play against the United States because it was decided to rely on the same eleven that had beaten Chile. The Belo Horizonte Stadium had been built specially for the World Cup, but naturally was nothing like the huge arena at Rio. It was a small ground, with a bumpy pitch. Dressing-room accommodation was poor, and the England team changed in the nearby Minas Athletic Club.

The Americans were favourites with the crowd from the start. I suppose it was just because they were the underdogs. Certainly, England couldn't get going that day, and the United States team was allowed to settle down, and play surprisingly good football. However, if England had found real form, I am sure we would have been two or three goals up in half-an-hour.

As it was, handicapped by the small ground and pitch, and not finding true form, we found ourselves behind five minutes before half-time when Gaetjens, the American centre-forward headed in a centre from the right wing. England were disturbed, but I hoped this goal would act as a pin-prick, and start the boys going, but it was not to be. No more goals were scored, and the craziest result of the series was flashed round the world—United States 1, England 0.

Folk back home were flabbergasted. We could hardly believe it was true, and our English friends of the mining camp, who sympathized with us, told us it would take years to live down this defeat among the Brazilians who worked with them. We felt we had let everybody down, but these things happen in sport, and I don't intend taking credit away from the Americans, who won on their merits that day, when I say I am sure England would beat them by three or four goals nine times out of ten.

It was a sad band of boys who gathered at what was really intended to be a victory party thrown by the Mine-owners. Little was said, but we we knew in our hearts the one thing we had never thought possible had come off.

But it is silly to cry over what can't be changed. So now it was Spain or bust! We flew back to Rio with the knowledge that we had to beat the Spaniards to have any chance of playing in the final groupings. A draw or defeat would mean our sudden return to England—a state of affairs that none of us had even anticipated. If we beat Spain we would be equal on points with them. This situation would entitle us to a second play-off with the Spaniards.

When the team to meet the Spain side was announced, there were four changes from the side beaten by America. I was recalled, Bill Eckersley, the Blackburn Rovers left-back, replaced Jack Aston, Eddie Baily, 'Spurs inside-left, took over from Wilf Mannion, and Jack Milburn was brought back at centre-forward to the exclusion of Roy Bentley. With myself on the right wing, Tom Finney went to outside-left with Jimmy Mullen dropping out.

We knew we were up against it, but somehow we thought we could pull it off. I thought England played pretty football, but, as at Belo Horizonte, goals would not come . . . partly because we were not shooting at our best, and partly because Spain's famous goalkeeper, Ramalets, excelled as he dived, jumped and threw himself at every shot.

A pity that Spain, who played some really good old-fashioned first-time football, should spoil their performance with some doubtful tactics. Twice I was pulled back by my shirt when passing a defender and Mortensen and Milburn were tripped up when going through. These fouls would have been certain penalties in England. There was also body-checking that was allowed by the Italian referee, Signor Galeati. The Spaniards used their hands freely in the second half, and kicked out of play late in the game. They were well satisfied because they had scored the only goal through their centre-forward, Zarra, soon after half-time. Not that time-wasting is any great crime. It happens every Saturday in our own League games.

And so, the worst had happened. England, the masters of Soccer, had failed even to qualify for the World Cup Finals. Even the Brazilians sympathized as they waved their handkerchiefs in the closing minutes and chanted " Adios ". This is a Brazilian custom when one of the teams is getting beaten in a competition.

Brazil, Spain, Sweden and Uruguay qualified for the finals, but we were flying home a rather sad party. The Brazilians routed Sweden 7—1 and beat Spain 6—1. It seemed they were the super team of the World Cup, but the trophy went to little Uruguay, who after drawing 2—2 with Spain, and beating Sweden 3—2 pipped Brazil 2—1 in the great Rio Stadium and so collected 5 points to Brazil's 4. There were tears and fists clenched to the Heavens after that result, because down Rio way they are a little more temperamental than ourselves, and they take defeat to heart.

The trip to Rio was a failure as far as English football was concerned, but at least we came through with our sportsmanship as high as ever. I never heard one real complaint from a colleague, or from Walter Winterbottom, Mr. Arthur Drewry or Sir Stanley Rous. It was good to know England could still take it.

South America thought we had had it after our poor showing in Rio, but that was not so, and some lost prestige was regained when in the most outstanding of the Festival of Britain internationals we defeated Argentina 2—1 at Wembley on May 9, 1951. Argentine held a 1—0 lead until near the end, but thanks to some fine fighting spirit by England and a couple of goals by Milburn and Mortensen, we retained our unbeaten record in spite of the brilliant if temperamental antics of goalkeeper Rugilo.

After returning from Brazil, I played for the F.A. team that had toured Canada against an England Rio XI at Stamford Bridge in September, and although we lost, I was chosen for England against Ireland at Belfast in October. We won 4—1 that day, but I wasn't chosen again for England until the Scotland match at Wembley on April 14, 1951—two weeks after I had appeared in the Cup Final against Newcastle United.

England had bad luck, because Wilf Mannion, who was my partner at inside-right fractured a cheek-bone after 11 minutes, and was carried off on a stretcher, taking no further part.

This ruined the game, and although we tried everything we knew with myself playing inside, we couldn't overcome the handicap, and so Scotland won 3—2.

CHAPTER XXIII

MIXED GRILL

I buy Parbleu. . . . I am selected for the Blackpool Illuminations. . . . Football characters. . . . The rat who would a-chewing go—and the booby prize. . . . Hugh O'Donnell plays in R.A.F. boots, and scores from twenty yards. . . . We get a lift—and we don't. . . . Alex James—the greatest. . . . Laughing with Frank Swift. . . . Blackpool's war-time team the best-ever. . . . Worst Man and Best Man to Ivor Powell.

THEY say variety is the spice of life. Well, I've tried many things outside of Soccer, an in 1949, I became a racehorse owner. It was while making a stage appearance in Hull, demonstrating tennis football that I received an invitation to visit Bill Hammett's stables at Beverley. Tom Moss and Wee Georgie Wood, who were appearing on the stage, were also invited. I have always had a fondness for animals, and after chatting with Mr. Hammett I asked him to buy a suitable horse for me at the Newmarket sales. Later that year Bill bought Parbleu, a five-year-old. I chose red, white and tangerine as my colours which, of course, was after Stoke City (red and white) and Blackpool (tangerine).

Parbleu won four times under my ownership, but not on any of these winning occasions was I present to lead him in. In all, Parbleu ran twelve races for me. He finished second four times, third on two occasions, and was twice unplaced.

We thought he had a good chance in the Liverpool Cup and the Manchester Handicap. Billy Thompson was engaged to ride at Liverpool, but to our disappointment, Parbleu finished last which was an unpleasant surprise, because he had been a consistent horse as his record showed. The following week he ran in the Manchester Handicap. Bill Hammett was puzzled by his disappointing form at Liverpool, and three days before the Handicap, Parbleu was given a trial at Beverley, and came through with flying colours. Billy Thompson was ill, and unable to take the saddle, so Geoff Littlewood was engaged. But I guess horses, like humans, are sometimes temperamental and not always up to the mark. Anyway, Parbleu was badly drawn near the outside and finished well down the course.

Some of my friends are jockeys. Great fellows like Gordon Richards, Bobby Jones, Billy Carr, Lew Jones and Billy Nevett, and many more. They are all keen football fans. But racing is a full-time job. You can't dabble with it at week-ends if you want to make a success of it, so in June, with some reluctance, I sold Parbleu. He was bought by Mrs. Houghton, and I hope she is well satisfied, because as I write this he has won four times for her.

I have been picked to represent England quite a few times, but a big surprise to me was when I was picked to switch on the 300,000 lamps for Blackpool's Festival Year illuminations in September, 1951. Just after the clock struck eight on September 7, standing on the steps of the Town Hall in Talbot Square I pulled the switch while a crowd of 8,000 people gathered for the ceremony.

The Corporation had promised sight-seers a special surprise. I certainly got one. A lit-up football appeared above my head, and then a representation of myself scoring a goal was shown in coloured lights. The goalkeeper was spreadeagled, and each time the ball entered the net the crowd cheered in good fun. Probably they were pulling my leg knowing that I don't score many goals. I was introduced by the Mayor, Councillor Joseph Hill, J.P., who told the onlookers: "Everybody in the universe ought to see Blackpool illuminations once. They are bigger, brighter and better than ever."

I endorse the Mayor's comments, and say that certainly every man, woman and child should see this great display of lights at least once in their lives. If it was a show put on in some other country, British people would go abroad just to see them.

I had to say a few words, and I reminded the onlookers that this was the third time I had stood on the Town Hall steps—twice before with the Blackpool team that had reached the Cup Final at Wembley, but had not been able to bring the Cup to Blackpool.

It was a happy night. Blackpool's Skylon with its 520 feet of lights could be seen miles away. Soon cars and coaches began to jam the promenades from the North to South shores. It was truly a wonderful sight.

I have had many laughs from football. Characters like Alex James,

Frank Swift, Ken Willingham, Bert Brown and " Jock " Dodds could earn fortunes on the stage as comedians if they so chose. Yet the funniest story I ever heard in football concerns Harry Sellars, former Stoke City left-half. Stoke were playing at Middlesbrough. The night before the game Harry and Bob McGrory, a member of the team at that time, shared a room together.

Bob was awakened in the night by a movement in the bedroom, and switched on the light just in time to catch a glimpse of a rat darting across the room with an object in its mouth, only to disappear behind the wainscoting. Bob jumped out of bed and shook Harry. Both players searched the bedroom, and then Harry shouted: "Hey, Bob, the so-and-so has taken my false teeth."

It was not any laughing matter for Harry, but Bob found it difficult to keep a straight face—especially when he recalled that the team had eaten cheese sandwiches that night! Harry complained to the hotel manager, who at first would not believe the story, but when finally convinced, paid Sellars £1 to replace the kidnapped dentures.

The sequel to the story is remarkable. Stoke were at Middlesbrough again two seasons later, and by this time I had come into the first team. Tom Mather arranged a whist-drive among the players on the Friday night with the promise of a " very special prize." Late that night when the cards were finished, Mr. Mather announced he had a booby prize for Harry Sellars. Believe it or not, wrapped up neatly in tissue paper and tied with ribbon were Harry's dentures!

The hotel had been redecorated and partly rebuilt. Workmen had found the dental-plate in a rat's nest behind the bedroom wall.

A hundred little incidents flash through my memory. Unimportant perhaps, but thoughts that can raise a smile at odd moments in the day, and, therefore, memories worth treasuring. I often chuckle when I think of " Jock " Dodds and Hugh O'Donnell, who shared " digs " at Blackpool early in the war. Both had been chosen for an R.A.F. unit match, but overslept. Following a loud banging on the front door, " Jock," sleepy-eyed and still in his pyjamas leaned out of the window. He soon woke up. The C.O. was outside the house. So was the bus with the other players sitting waiting. Jock came down partly dressed and Hugh O'Donnell played in his R.A.F. boots, and scored a smashing goal from twenty yards out.

One of my earliest trips abroad was when Stoke City played in Holland. I was only eighteen, and easily impressed. The Dutch teams played with white footballs. Everybody in Holland seemed to possess a bicycle, because there were thousands lined up outside the ground. I was fascinated by the road-sweepers who smoked impressive cigars that were hardly pick-ups!

I have seldom been late for a game, but in war-time I had one or two close shaves. On Boxing Day, 1944, the R.A.F. were due to play the Army at Leeds. A fog came down. Dodds and I were held up, and jumped out of the train at Leeds station five minutes before the kick-off—still some way from the ground.

There was a considerable queue for taxis outside the station, but Jock and I having to "report for duty" at three o'clock, rushed up to the first taxi shouting: "Footballers! We've got to get to the ground in five minutes." Perhaps the onlookers were too surprised to protest, but there was not any opposition, and we changed our boots and stockings in the taxi. As we arrived at the ground the R.A.F. team with nine players walked out followed by the Army. "The King" was being played while we were completing our change of clothes, but we ran on the field just in time for the kick-off. Sad ending is we were beaten.

After another R.A.F.—Army game at Edinburgh, Peter Doherty and I were attempting to catch an early train back to Blackpool. We had arranged for a taxi to be waiting outside the entrance to the dressing-rooms immediately the match was over. Half dressed, we dashed out, but this was one driver who obviously was not a football fan, and, after waiting five minutes, we knew we had had it. Peter spotted an R.A.F. car waiting. An attractive W.A.A.F. was sitting at the wheel, and we threw ourselves on her mercy, but she explained the C.O.—a group Captain—would be coming out of the club in ten minutes or so. Peter appealed again, and won. She told us to jump in, warning us that we would probably get her shot if her C.O. ever found out We thought everything was lovely, but a gruff voice shouted: "Get out!" It was the Group Captain who had arrived sooner than expected. We appealed to him, but he gave Peter, myself and the unfortunate W.A.A.F. a dressing-down. When we explained the whole incident was entirely our fault he ignored us completely. Fortunately a kindly Scotsman, who witnessed the scene volunteered to drive us to Princes Street Station, and we just made the train.

Alex James was the greatest footballer I ever saw. His dribbling was superb. It was not always what he did, but what he did not do that caused so much trouble to opposing defences. The bushy eyebrows and spud nose would always be turning up in places least expected. Alex was a genius of tactics. I recall a Stoke-Arsenal game. Alex was at inside-left as usual, and Frankie Soo had been given special instructions to watch the Arsenal wizard. As the teams lined up for the kick-off Alex suddenly switched to inside-right, completely disrupting our pre-match plans. He said later that having taken one look at Frankie at the line-up, he sensed Soo had had special instructions to concentrate on marking him. Hence the quick decision to switch to inside-right.

Alex is certainly a character—one of the few remaining from the older school. He is still the best-known footballer in Britain, although he has been out of the game fifteen years. Wherever he goes his merry face is recognized. I once walked with him along Whitehall in search of a cab. Alex hailed an approaching taxi, and from thirty yards' distance the driver's face lit up: "Where to, Alex?" he asked, "Highbury Corner?" I might have been carrying Alex's bag for all the driver cared.

Frank Swift can always raise a laugh. Frank has probably the biggest hands and feet in the game. He used to be useful with his fists as an amateur, and, who knows, we might have had a heavyweight champ called "Swift," had big Frank not had such a passion to be a goalkeeper.

Swift once arrived at Stoke with the Manchester City team, only to discover in the dressing-room that he had packed two right boots. He appealed to me, and I sent my brother Ronnie in a taxi to my sports shop to see if we had a pair of football boots large enough to fit Frank. It was, of course, a hopeless journey so Frank kept goal in two right boots.

When a Combined Services team flew in a mist from France towards the end of the war, we learned from the pilot on landing that we had missed colliding with another plane by fifteen yards over the Channel. Big Frank immediately fell on his face kissing the ground in "Praise be to Allah" style.

Swift has cheered up many a losing team with his "fish and chips" act which he puts over really well, and he soon has the company in fits imitating a lady having trouble with a two-way stretch.

Stan Cullis is one of the greatest centre-half-backs I have played with. When he captained the England team during the war he was really superb.

I am often asked to pick a best-ever football team, but I have refrained, and shall continue to refrain because I think comparisons between players of different periods are absurd. It is like arguing that Dempsey was a better fighter than Sullivan, or that Louis would have beaten Dempsey. One could argue for a year, without proving a point.

I will, however, name the best team in which I have ever played—the Blackpool war-time eleven that won the League North Cup, beating Sheffield Wednesday in May, 1943, and went on to beat Arsenal (who had won the South Cup) 4—2, at Stamford Bridge

The team was: Savage (Queen of the South), Pope (Hearts), Sam Jones, Farrow, Hayward, Johnston, Matthews (Stoke), Dix ('Spurs),

IN ROOM 142

Author gives his most important autograph in room of Glasgow Hotel. He has just signed for Blackpool after the Great Britain v. Rest of Europe game. Blackpool manager Joe Smith and Stoke manager Bob McGrory stand behind Matthews. Mr. Harry Evans, now chairman of Blackpool, is on the right

MEETING THE LATE KING GEORGE VI BEFORE THE 1948 CUP FINAL

Dodds, Finan, Burbanks (Sunderland). (Hubbick played at left-back against Arsenal).

George Farrow, the Blackpool right-half, was one of the greatest footballers who never played for England. I have not played in front of a better wing-half.

I smile when I look back on my early days with the R.A.F. at Blackpool. The N.C.O., Sergeant Powell—Ivor Powell, the former Queen's Park Rangers', Aston Villa and Welsh International wing-half—put our flight through its paces. For five days I was just 1361317 to him. Later we became good friends, and I was Best Man at his wedding. I had once been his Worst Man.

Since moving to Blackpool, I have made many friends—far too many to mention here because the list would go into pages, but the man who helped me more than anyone was the late Colonel W. Parkinson, chairman of Blackpool F.C. It was Colonel Parkinson who asked me to play for Blackpool when I first arrived there as an R.A.F. recruit.

In spite of past differences between players and the Football League over minimum and maximum salaries, all is now well because in this great national game of ours no matter what the difference between club and player may be, there is only one thing in the player's mind when he gets on the field—and that is to help beat the opposition. A player's life is not all honey, but I have yet to meet the professional footballer who would change his career if he was given his life over again.

We need more young stars, because the war hit us more than any other country, but they will come as sure as night follows day. There is a potential Alex James, another Tommy Lawton, a Cliff Bastin playing on some small heath or kicking a brick in some back street.

They will be spotted and coached, and when I am sitting back with happy memories the masses will be comparing these kids, unknown to-day, with former great Masters of a great Art—Association Football.

CHAPTER XXIV

LUCK—GOOD AND BAD

Tom Finney takes his chance. . . . And the band played "God Save the King"—in Dublin. . . . Passed over by England. . . . Finney's turn of bad luck. . . . Enter Billy Steele. . . . The crazy age of transfer fees. . . . Phantom Whistle. . . . All's well that ends well.

I ONCE got back into the England team early in my international career through the bad luck of another player—Ralph Birkett who, after being selected to play on the right wing against Germany at Tottenham in 1935, had to drop out through injury. More than ten years later I lost my place for a similar reason. After an unbroken run as England's outside-right during which time I managed to escape injury my luck turned.

The streak of bad luck which dogged me began in January, 1946, when I went down with 'flu and almost missed my record-breaking forty-fourth apearance for England against Belgium at Wembley. Two months later I tore the ligaments of my knee when playing as a guest for Blackpool, and this injury caused me to cry off after being selected to play against Scotland at Hampden Park.

I played against Switzerland and France in the 1945–46 season, which took me within reach of Billy Meredith's record of 51 international appearances. Meredith's record is wonderful because he gained fifty-one "caps" in full internationals. "Caps" were not awarded during the war, and I can only claim thirty-three "caps."

I was chosen for the first two international games of the 1946–47 season—against Ireland at Belfast on September 28, and against Eire in Dublin two days later. Apart from improving my record I was particularly anxious to play in the Dublin game, because it was the first appearance of an English eleven in that city since 1912.

My luck was out, and I injured my knee slightly in the first few games of the season, which necessitated my dropping out of the trial game between an F.A. XI and a combined Services team at Nottingham, staged in aid of Willie Hall. I could not take any chances, and did not return to the Stoke City side until September 21, when we played Manchester United. Quite early on I went to sprint for the ball, and tore a muscle behind my right knee. I had never known such a run of bad luck in my career, and although I spent Sunday massaging the knee I knew deep down inside me I should have to cry off. Next morning my fears were confirmed, and I had to notify the F.A. I was unfit to sail to Belfast the following Wednesday.

This was a lucky break for Tom Finney, who had been included in the reserves. He automatically took my place—and at the right time, too, because "caps" were awarded to players for the first time since April, 1939. Furthermore, the clever Preston winger kept me out of the England team for several games after I had recovered from my leg injury.

There were several newcomers in the side besides Finney. Harry Cockburn, young Manchester United left-half, Wilf Mannion, Middlesbrough inside-left, and Langton, the Blackburn Rovers left-winger, now playing for Bolton, were included. Mannion had played for England early in the war, but had been overseas for several years.

While I was nursing my injured right knee at Blackpool, Swift (Manchester City), Scott (Arsenal), Hardwick (Middlesbrough), Wright (Wolverhampton Wanderers), Franklin (Stoke City), Cockburn (Manchester United), Finney (Preston North End), Carter (Derby County), Lawton (Chelsea), Mannion (Middlesbrough), Langton (Blackburn Rovers) and Welsh (Charlton), Shimwell (Sheffield United) and Hancocks (Wolverhapton Wanderers) as reserves, sailed for Belfast.

I sat in my hotel feeling a little sorry for myself, and thought of the corresponding trip in September, 1945 when we played the first international after the war, against Ireland at Belfast. On that occasion there had been some excitement when the pilot engine of the train in which most of the Northern players were travelling left the line near Kendal.

Travelling with me were Frank Swift, Joe Mercer, Frank Soo, Neil Franklin, Billy Watson and "Raich" Carter, but we were all sleeping and knew nothing of the incident until we arrived at Stranraer many hours late. The rest of the party, travelling from London, were relieved to know we were safe, and were a little disappointed when we could not relate any details of the mishap. While we slept we had been shunted on to a siding, blissfully unaware of what might have been a sticky business.

But back to the later Irish trip. On the Saturday I listened to the broadcast of the first match against Ireland. When Carter crashed in a left-footed shot to put England a goal up in the first minute, it was obvious that the locals were booked for defeat. That's how it worked out, and the large crowd that had swarmed on to the pitch before the game, and only returned to the terraces when a voice through the loud-speakers threatened that the game would be abandoned unless the pitch was cleared, was reduced to silence as England went on to register a 7—2 victory. Finney had a good game, and so did Carter, and the newspaper accounts warned me I would have a job to get back into the England team.

The same England team tackled Eire at Dolymount Park on the Monday. This must have been a wonderful sight. 32,000 Southern Irishmen standing bareheaded while the band played "God Save the King," and then the English team and officials standing to attention while Eire's national anthem—"The Soldier's Song" was played. While Irish pipers marched up and down blowing their lungs out playing the song of the rebels "The Wearing of the Green," a Union Jack floated at one end of the ground. All of which proves what a great binder is sport. Here we had complete friendship between England and Ireland. Yet if someone had started talking politics or religion, it might have ended in free fights all round.

The match itself proved a big surprise. Following England's easy win in Belfast an even bigger walk-over was expected against the Eire side, but the Irishmen fought with such spirit that in the end England were, according to reports, lucky to win. It was Tom Finney who scored the only goal in the game, eight minutes from time.

I spoke to several of the players on their return, and they admitted that the enthusiasm of the Irish players plus the roaring of the crowd had helped to put the England team out of their stride. Also, the smallness of the ground had been a handicap to the Englishmen.

Doctor Kevin O'Flanagan, Arsenal's amateur forward, and his brother Michael, had supplied the dash while Alec Stevenson and Tommy Eglington, the Everton left-wing, supplied the skill. Stevenson almost spoiled England's record when fifteen minutes from time he sent in a great thirty yard drive that struck the cross-bar, and rebounded to be cleared by Laurie Scott.

The excited Irish crowd had kept up an incessant cheer that was a miniature Hampden Roar, but when Finney scored for England there was complete silence. The Irishmen felt they had been wronged, and according to reporters at the game this was an occasion when Ireland had every right to complain of injustice.

My injury meant the end of any ambitions I had of beating the Meredith record that season. In fact, I began to wonder if I would ever achieve it, because several of the football writers openly declared Finney had come to stay. Naturally, I had no grouse against Finney, a fine footballer, but I did curse my bad luck, because I do not think I would have been dropped without injury.

But the luck goes round. Tom Finney has had his run of bad luck with injuries which kept him out of quite a few games in the

1951–52 season. He missed the representative match between Wales and the United Kingdom at Cardiff through injury. And he must have been even more disappointed when he pulled a thigh muscle when playing for Preston against Chelsea at Stamford Bridge in November 1951—only four days before he was to play for England against Austria at Wembley in one of the most ballyhooed international matches of recent years.

With the whole football press running out of adjectives in praise of the Austrians, this obviously was to be a great prestige match for England. Our unbeaten record at home was still intact. Would the Austrians be the first foreign side to bring English Soccer to its knees on British soil? Or would England show that we could still hold our heads high as the masters? These were some of the controversial questions the newspapers were asking, and naturally Tom Finney, and any other footballer with half a chance, wanted to play in this important match.

Finney had intended to stay in London after the Chelsea match, and join up with the rest of the England party at their headquarters at Hendon, but when he pulled a muscle behind his right knee after sixty minutes' play, he made up his mind there and then to travel back to Preston and get treatment from Desmond Coupe, North End's blind physiotherapist, who lost his sight in a naval action in the Adriatic.

Finney and the rest of his team have great faith in Desmond's hands, but Tom was over-optimistic, because I know from painful experience that when you get a badly pulled muscle nature demands time to allow it to mend. Treatment, of course, helps, but you can't rush these jobs.

Tom found this out to his regret and had to cry off. This gave Arthur Milton, Arsenal's right-winger and Gloucestershire cricketer, his first "cap" for England. Arthur is a most promising winger, but perhaps the Wembley occasion was too much for him, because he never found his best club form. However, Milton is likely to play for England again.

England's next international after that Eire game in Dublin was against Wales at Manchester in November, and controversy raged in the Press and in football circles. "Matthews or Finney?" Or, as some of the bright boys asked, "Is Matthews Finis?"

When the England team was announced my name was missing, and the selectors had decided to stand by Finney who had justified himself in the matches in Belfast and Dublin less than two months earlier. Quite honestly, I was disappointed, but that was all. I was now tasting some of the sour grapes of football, having tasted many of the sweeter fruits. I felt the publicity given to my trouble with Stoke City was not doing me any good. In addition, I was a little hurt by the fickleness of the folk who one minute professed to be my friends, and were now spreading it abroad that I was out for good.

I must confess, however, it began to look that way. I travelled from Blackpool to Maine Road to watch the game against Wales, and once more renewed my acquaintance with Billy Meredith, who sportingly wished me luck in overhauling his record, and told me not to worry unduly. " You'll be back before the season is out, Stanley," whispered the wonderful old man.

But England beat Wales 3—0 that day, and the Meredith goal began to fade further from my reach when two weeks later I was again passed over for the England-Holland game at Huddersfield. The amateur Dutch XI was completely outclassed and beaten 8—2. Only Wilkes and Smit in the Dutch forward line, and goalkeeper, Praak, seemed to settle down on the rain-soaked pitch which made the going too heavy for the Dutch boys. England did not have another fixture until the Scotland game at Wembley on April 12, 1947. Although I was recalled for this game, which was drawn 1—1, it was not a good day for the England team as a whole—and particularly myself.

I recall the game for two particular incidents. Firstly, that Billy Steel made his debut for Scotland, and although Billy did not score he was so successful that much of the credit for Scotland's fine display was attributed to him. In addition, he caused two sensations a month later. (1) He was chosen out of the four countries to represent Great Britain against The Rest of Europe at Hampden. (2) He was transferred from Greenock Morton to Derby County for £15,500, which was the first post-war transfer figure to beat the £14,000 paid to Wolves by Arsenal for Bryn Jones in 1938. Since Billy Steel's transfer, prices have rocketed to such fantastic figures that the sum paid for Steel has been more than doubled. In fact, we reached Soccer inflation, in my opinion, when Sheffield Wednesday paid £34,000 for Jackie Sewell of Notts County in March 1951.

More than twenty players have been transferred for a higher fee than that £15,500 Derby County paid to Morton for Steel. Derby, of course, made a profit when following pressure from Billy himself they transferred him to Dundee in 1950 for £17,500. Just take a look at some of these figures, and you'll be inclined to agree with me, I feel sure, that the transfer market lost all sense of proportion after the war:

Jackie Sewell transferred to Shef. Wed. from Notts Co., £34,000

Trevor Ford transferred to Sunderland from Aston Villa, £29,500

Eddie Quigley transferred to Preston from Shef. Wed., £26,500

Allan Brown transferred to Blackpool from East Fife, £26,000

There are several players who were transferred for £25,000, and a good list between that figure and £20,000. Leon Leuty, the Notts County centre-half, has figured in transfer fees amounting to £45,000. Bradford paid £20,000 to Derby County for Leuty's signature in March 1950, and Notts County gave Bradford £25,000 for him six months later.

I wonder what old Alf Common would think about it now, because there was quite a to-do in 1905 when Middlesbrough paid Sunderland £1,000 for his signature—the first-ever four-figure transfer fee in football!

But back to Wembley and the second remarkable incident. Scotland scored through McLaren in the fifteenth minute, and played well enough to be two or three goals up at half-time instead of leading 1—0. There was not any doubt that England had to struggle before "Raich" Carter equalized in the second-half. Oddly enough, Carter went through again and could have given England a win against the run of the play. He took a through pass neatly, and stood unchallenged apart from the Scottish goalkeeper, Miller. To the astonishment of a 99,000 crowd, he pulled up, trapping the ball, and looking round at the French referee, M. de la Salle, who promptly and excitedly waved play on, but the chance was gone.

Carter believed he had been given off-side, but the whistle had not come from the referee, but a man in the crowd!

I had not been able to consolidate my position at outside-right, and the selectors recalled Finney for the match against France at Highbury a few weeks later. Remembering that France had played wonderful football when holding us to a 2—2 draw at Wembley in 1945, and had beaten us 2—1 in Paris in 1946, England expected tougher opposition this time, but played well to win 3—0, although the French were handicapped when Gregoire, their centre-half, collided with Tommy Lawton, and went on the wing. Both Gregoire and Lawton had to leave the field to have stitches in their cuts.

The season which had been extended was now almost over, and I began to look back on it as the unluckiest in my career. There had been the injury which kept me out of the England team at the start of the season in Ireland. There had been the trouble at Stoke, and now I was unsettled in the England team.

But all is well that ends well, and my biggest thrill for a long, long time followed when I was honoured to play for Great Britain against the Rest of Europe at Hampden the week after England had beaten France. Nine years earlier I had played for England against the Rest of Europe at Highbury, but this was more important because our team was to be chosen from England, Ireland, Scotland and Wales. It was a special match arranged to celebrate the return of the Football

Association to the Federation International Football Association after a break of eighteen years.

After this I was included in the F.A. party to tour Switzerland and Portugal the same month, and was fortunate enough to be chosen for England in all the internationals in the 1947–48 season. The only game I missed was against Sweden at Highbury in November, when I had to call off at the last minute owing to a leg injury.

So you see, it is wise to learn to take the good luck with the bad. I am a lucky man to have had the opportunity of at last beating the Meredith record, having made 64 international appearances up to the end of the 1950–51 season.

What the future holds I do not know. I hope to have another two years in top-class football, but I make no predictions. I am encouraged by the fact that Meredith, the daddy of all wingers, turned out for Manchester City in an F.A. cup-tie in the 1923–24 season when he was approaching fifty!

CHAPTER XXV

I SIGN FOR BLACKPOOL

More trouble at Stoke. . . . Directors agree to release me. . . . Secrecy, but someone talked. . . . Midnight transfer. . . . Babel United.

I BECAME a Blackpool player a few minutes before midnight on May 10, 1947—some seven hours after I had helped Great Britain defeat the Rest of Europe 6—1. I signed the necessary forms in the room of my Glasgow hotel. Blackpool, who were represented by Messrs. Harry Evans, vice-chairman at this time, and Joe Smith, the manager, handed a cheque for £11,500 to Stoke City, represented by Messrs. Enshall, Burton (directors) and Bob McGrory. I said earlier that I have never considered myself to be worth £20,000. I repeat this, but emphasize that regarding my own transfer I made it quite clear that I was not open to go to any club, because I wanted to go to Blackpool in order to look after my hotel.

Although the blow-up between Stoke and myself in the October had been smoothed out following the special meeting with the directors things were never quite the same, and I was not happy at Stoke. In addition, I was tied up with my business in Blackpool, which remains important to me when my playing days are over.

The trouble which had been simmering for some little time came to the boil over the three Easter holiday games. Stoke were due at Grimsby on Good Friday, at home to Huddersfield on the Saturday, and at home to Grimsby again on Easter Monday. In view of the fact I was due to play for England against Scotland at Wembley the following Saturday I made a special request to miss travelling to Grimsby for the game on Good Friday. Bob McGrory agreed, but said that he would expect me to be at Stoke on Saturday to play against Huddersfield, and, naturally, I assured him I would be there.

Stoke gained a comfortable win at Grimsby. On the Friday night I drove from Blackpool to Stoke, and called at the Stoke manager's office at ten-thirty on Saturday morning. In view of Stoke's convincing win at Grimsby I realised Bob McGrory might want to stick to a winning team, and was prepared to co-operate. But the manager said he wanted me to play, and to be at the ground at the usual time. Yet, when I arrived at the Victoria Ground forty-five minutes before the kick-off I was told my services were not required, as Stoke were, after all, relying on a winning team. That was fair enough, but surely I could have been told this in a straightforward manner in the morning. Stoke beat Huddersfield, and I was informed the same winning team would be fielded against Grimsby at Stoke on Easter Monday, which seemed sound policy to me.

The following Saturday I played for England against Scotland, and the same day Stoke kept up their winning sequence, winning at Blackpool. And so to the following Saturday with Stoke City at home to Brentford. On the Wednesday before the game my name was included among six forwards. So I reported at Stoke on the Saturday morning to learn I was to play. George Mountford, who had been successfully holding the outside-right berth, moved to inside-right to partner me. But I learned afterwards the only reason I was included was that a vacancy had occurred because another player was unfit. The directors denied this, but the evidence of the Stoke City programme for the Brentford game satisfied me that it was the original intention not to play me.

I was fed up. Accuse me of being temperamental, if you like, but I must emphasize that in order to play on top form every footballer must have the confidence of his club—the directors, the manager and the other players—behind him. If he doesn't get it his own confidence is undermined and his game deteriorates. I was unhappy at the way I was being treated. So I asked to meet the directors once more, and the meeting was fixed for April 23.

At this meeting I told the Stoke directors of my grievances and that my life was being made unhappy by the rumours that were going around. One paper had accused me of refusing to play on the Good Friday, and that, as a result, disciplinary measures were taken against me and I was dropped for the remaining Easter games. This, as I have explained, was not true. Another announcement stated that I would have to play inside-right to Mountford. This again was untrue, but it was all unsettling.

The directors were sympathetic and offered to do what they could to avoid my being unsettled, but I was convinced in my own mind that the trouble would start up again in the near future, so I asked for a transfer. This was at first refused, but when I explained I wanted to get to Blackpool to look after my hotel, and to avoid the continual travelling to Stoke, which rendered even home fixtures as away games to me, the directors reconsidered their decision, and agreed to let me go to Blackpool.

A condition of secrecy was made. Nothing of the meeting should be whispered outside, and certainly not to the Press. I should remain a Stoke player until the end of the season, and the negotiations with Blackpool would be opened in July. Alderman Harry Booth, the chairman, bound us all to secrecy, and I was happy that the meeting ended in handshakes all round.

But somebody broke his word, and spoke out of turn, and when a few days later I left with the Football League XI to play in Ireland, reporters were waiting for me at the boat to get my reactions to the news which I still believed to be secret. I kept my bargain, and refused to comment, but in Ireland next day some of the papers carried the story that I had asked for a transfer, plus speculations and exaggerations. One version was that I had handed the directors an ultimatum, and had told them that if they refused to transfer me to Blackpool I intended quitting football, and that Stoke City would lose a five-figure transfer fee. That was not only untrue, but most damaging to my reputation as a sportsman. On my return from Ireland insulting letters from a few Stoke supporters who had the facts completely wrong were waiting for me. I was accused of being swollen-headed, and a bad sportsman. This could not have happened had not somebody present at the meeting between the Stoke directors and myself spoken out of turn. It certainly made my private life a misery with more publicity.

The breaking of the news speeded up my transfer to Blackpool. The late Colonel Parkinson, then chairman of Blackpool, began negotiations, which were held up by Stoke asking for considerably more than they eventually received. Colonel Parkinson made it clear that as I had made the request to go to Blackpool, Stoke should be reasonable about it. He was not prepared to pay a record fee in view of the fact that no other clubs were bidding against Blackpool.

The Stoke and Blackpool officials met in Glasgow a few days later to try to come to terms. Meantime, I was resting quietly with the

Great Britain team at beautiful but lonely Aberfoyle, lying at the foot of the Trossachs, and overlooking Loch Ard. At one time the negotiations looked like breaking down, but the late Sir Francis Joseph, the Stoke City president, who I know had always had my interest at heart, stepped in, and I believe, the £11,500 fee was agreed upon the night before the Hampden match, although I did not actually sign until near midnight the following night.

I was certainly relieved when it all went through so smoothly, and so happily. Sir Francis Joseph took me aside, and wished me all the luck in the world with my new club, a great gesture from a great man, whose death has left football poorer, and has deprived me of a friend.

And now a word or two about the remarkable Hampden match. I say remarkable because it was a terrific achievement to get together eleven players nearly all speaking a different language, and asking them to work in harmony. Although Britain won 6—1, the European side played better than could be expected considering the handicap they were up against. Obviously, Sweden, France or Italy would have offered stronger resistance than this eleven of Babel United.

Karel Lotsy, the Dutchman, had the task of looking after this League of Nations football team. Jack Carey, the Manchester United and Irish international right back, was chosen as skipper of the Rest of Europe. Carey agreed to play at right half, a position in which he often played for Manchester United. Jack can speak one or two languages himself, but he is quite a philosopher, and he took the training at Troon, Ayrshire, all in good part. The good-humoured Irishman had a little fun of his own, too. On more than one occasion he addressed his foreign colleagues as "sons of guns," and they smilingly accepted Jack's wisecracks as compliments.

It was quite a performance to satisfy all the foreign officials and players present. In fact, some of the selectors at Troon left the room after finally picking the Rest of Europe team, and declared: "Never again."

The players had to be fed suitably. It wasn't a simple task. For instance, Da Rui, the pint-sized French goalkeeper, was fond of wine with many lumps of sugar in his glass. On one occasion he had twenty lumps, and argued it was essential for his stamina. Some requested garlic, others steaks, and others wanted special soups. Carey had simple tastes. He relied mainly on toast and fish.

But to the match itself. It had been decided that the Great Britain team should wear dark-blue jerseys, and the Rest of Europe chose Cambridge blue. We lined up like this:

Great Britain: Swift (Manchester City and England), Hardwick (Middlesbrough and England) (captain), Hughes (Birmingham and

Wales), Macaulay (Brentford and Scotland), Vernon (West Bromwich Albion and Ireland), Burgess (Tottenham Hotspur and Wales), Matthews (Stoke City and England), Mannion (Middlesbrough and England), Lawton (Chelsea and England), Steel (Greenock Morton and Scotland), Liddell (Liverpool and Scotland).

Rest of Europe: Da Rui (France), Peterson (Denmark), Steffen (Switzerland), Carey (Eire) (captain), Parola (Italy), Ludl (Czechoslovakia), Lemberechts (Belgium), Gren (Sweden), Nordahl (Sweden), Wilkes (Holland), Praest (Denmark).

We went off on the beam that day, and I sensed we were in for an easy victory in the first few minutes. Wilf Mannion, who had been switched from his usual position of inside-left in the England team to inside-right, kept me well supplied with passes in the first half, in which the British forward line moved in complete harmony.

On the run of play we should have been more than one up after twenty minutes when Mannion scored. Yet, oddly, we were pegged back again in a few minutes when Praest, the Danish left-winger, dribbled with great skill, rounded Hardwick, and passed to Gundar Nordahl, the Swedish fireman, who later went to Italy, to equalize from a few yards out.

Europe had fought back well, but we were never in any danger. Mannion gave us the lead again from a penalty soon afterwards, following an incident in which Ludl, the Czech left-half, had prevented an almost certain goal when he diverted a Mannion drive with his hand. After this it was easy. Billy Steel beat three Europeans and surprised everyone, including his own colleagues, by scoring from best part of thirty yards out. We all expected him to make a pass, and so did Da Rui, who dived seconds too late. I am sure this goal of Steel's put another £2,000 on his transfer fee. Middlesbrough and Liverpool officials were in Glasgow hoping to bring off a coup, but so many other clubs were impressed by this goal, and Steel's general performance, that they began bidding, and Derby County finally clinched the Morton inside forward's signature at a cost of £15,500.

Then Tommy Lawton came into the picture adding two second-half goals—one a perfect header from my centre. Britain's sixth and last goal was turned into his own net by Parola, the Italian centre-half, who in the briefest of pants had played great football. It was a stroke of bad luck on his part.

I think I can safely say that the 134,000 who saw this unique match at Hampden will agree with me that the entertainment was good, and, what is more important, the sportsmanship was wonderful. I don't recall a serious foul in the game. But the game, as an international, was not taken too seriously, and I doubt if the European countries that took part would agree to another match of this kind. Football is essentially a team game, and strangers cannot be expected to blend in such short time.

For me this day was an end of a perfect season. After the ill-luck that had dogged me from the opening weeks of the season I was satisfied that I had had a reasonably good match and with my future at Blackpool being settled that night I slept undisturbed for the first night in many weeks.

CHAPTER XXVI

A DIFFERENT LISBON STORY

Matthews—of Blackpool. . . . Switzerland spoil an England record. . . . Millionaire's playground again. . . . We get a ticket, but refuse it. . . . We refuse a small ball, but get it. . . . The England machine.

FIVE days after the Great Britain *v.* Rest of Europe game I set off with sixteen players in the England party to fly to Switzerland and Portugal. It was the first time I was to represent England as a Blackpool player, and I can tell you it took me some time to get used to being referred to as " Matthews of Blackpool," having played with Stoke City for seventeen years. I also felt happy being back in the England party after an uncertain season in international football.

In war-time football I had flown with R.A.F. teams, and had previously flown to Lisbon when the R.A.F. played the Portuguese Army in 1946. But this was the first occasion the Football Association flew an expensive party of footballers as far as Switzerland, on to Portugal, and back to London. I have always enjoyed my visits to Switzerland, and this trip lived up to expectations from the moment we arrived at our Zürich headquarters at the Dolder Grand Hotel and I noticed with delight that the hotel had its own golf course.

Although my old friendly rival, Tom Finney, travelled with the party he did not play against Switzerland, and the England team lined up like this: Swift (Manchester City), Scott (Arsenal), Hardwick (Middlesbrough) (captain), Wright (Wolves), Franklin (Stoke City), Lowe, E. (Aston Villa), Matthews (Blackpool), Carter (Derby County), Lawton (Chelsea), Mannion (Middlesbrough), Langton (Blackburn Rovers).

There isn't much I can say about this game—except that we lost 1—0 to the delight of 34,000 Swiss fans, and to the disappointment of England, who had not lost a match in the 1946–47 season. But let me say here that the Swiss, taking advantage of the small ground, deserved their victory—the result of a goal by their outside-left Fatton from a pass by Amado midway through the first half.

Naturally, it was not a good day for England. We had our chances in the first half, but did not take them, and once the determined Switzerland team settled down the players became more and more confident, and their tackling was always first-time stuff. From Zürich we moved on to Geneva for a match against the Swiss " B " team. There were five changes, and I was rested. Although this was not an international, and the game ended in a draw there was some high feeling towards the end of the game when Zanetti, the Swiss centre-forward, fell over, and a couple of bottles were thrown on the pitch. Fortunately, nothing worse developed, and we left Switzerland bound for Portugal with only good-will and friendship behind us.

And so next morning we flew to Portugal, which for me was to be the second chapter of my Lisbon Story—altogether a different Lisbon story to 1946 when the Portuguese Army had held the football strength of the R.A.F. to a draw.

We had a good journey to Lisbon, and from the airport drove some eight miles to Estoril to our headquarters at a luxurious hotel. The Portuguese are rightly proud of Estoril with its white buildings, exquisite display of geraniums and palm trees with stubby trunks that make them look like gigantic pineapples. The gardens are the finest I have ever seen, and are one mass of colour and perfume from the sea-front up to the Casino where poker-faced men and women sit for hours at the roulette and dice tables giving the inquisitive onlooker the impression that they are doing anything but enjoying themselves.

Add to the beauty of the lay-out of Estoril a blue sky and a blue sea, and you can understand perhaps why all football teams bound for Portugal are sent to this millionaire's playground. But there are some peculiar customs in Portugal that puzzled me. For instance, on the beach a man is not allowed to wear bathing trunks only. He must wear a singlet, and when some of the England party went in bathing we had the Portuguese police coming on to the beach trying to explain that we couldn't do this sort of thing there.

I was also astonished in Lisbon to learn that one is not allowed to use a cigarette lighter in the street without a licence. I believe this is due to the fact that the match industry is government controlled, and the government accordingly protects the match business. Pedestrians must observe the street crossings and if you break this rule a policeman comes up and fines you right away. He gives you a ticket, and you pay him the necessary escudos on the spot. I recall an amusing incident when I was strolling with an English friend, and we broke this traffic rule. A policeman came up to us excitedly with a ticket, and my friend kept saying "No! No!", at the same time pushing the ticket back in the infuriated policeman's hand. My friend thought he was being sold one of the lottery tickets which the Portuguese Government allow to be sold in the streets! Fortunately for us, the policeman was a good sportsman, and when he learned we were with the English football party he let us off with, what I imagined to be, a caution. Anyway, we observed the traffic rules after this.

Every Sunday in Lisbon they hold the bullfights at the impressive red-bricked bull-ring. Unlike in Spain, the bulls are not killed off in Portugal. Although I personally do not approve of bullfighting I must confess the skill of the matadors and the horsemanship is to be admired. The crowd certainly appreciate all the finer points, and if a matador gives the bull too wide a berth when tempting him with the red lining of his cloak the spectators whistle him off.

But back to football. We were driven from our hotel to visit the National Stadium. I, of course, had played there before, and so had Laurie Scott and Neil Franklin, who were members of the R.A.F. team. Yet I found myself more impressed than before. This time we approached the stadium from a different entrance, and noticed the station built so that thousands of Portuguese fans can be driven right up to the entrance of the stadium, and can be back in Lisbon less than thirty minutes from the end of the game.

A member of the Portuguese F.A. told me this white-marbled stadium cost nearly £350,000 to build, and was built at a time when there was unemployment. As the white marble comes from Portugal it was built cheaply. To erect a similar stadium in England, which would mean importing this marble, it would cost at least a million pounds. The Portuguese fan is not used to standing. He sits through the game on the white marble, but there are not any covered stands, and, of course, with almost perpetual sunshine he seldom requires cover. There is one beautiful white balcony with extravagant pillars at the back of the stadium. This is reserved for the President and his friends.

The pitch is the finest not only in Portugal but probably in the world. It is every bit up to the standard of Wembley, and is of Cumberland turf brought from Britain. This show piece is treasured by the Portuguese, and only special matches are played on it.

Before the F.A. selectors could pick our team they had to await reports on Phil Taylor, the Liverpool wing-half, Bobby Langton, Blackburn's left-winger, both injured in the Geneva game, and Neil Franklin who was doubtful about his ankle. All had treatment from Walter Max, physiotherapist of the England team, but after taking advice from Walter Winterbottom, the F.A. team-manager, the selectors decided that only Franklin was fit to play. So Tom Finney was selected for the first time at outside left in place of Langton, and Stan Mortensen was brought in to partner me at inside-right. The teams lined up:

Portugal: Azevedo, Cardozo, Feliciano, Amaro, Moreira, Ferreira, Correira, Araujo, Peyroteo, Travasos, Rogerio.

England: Swift (Manchester City), Scott (Arsenal), Hardwick (Middlesbrough) (captain), Wright (Wolverhampton Wanderers), Franklin (Stoke City), Lowe, E. (Aston Villa), Matthews (Blackpool), Mortensen (Blackpool), Lawton (Chelsea), Mannion (Middlesbrough), Finney (Preston North End).

Without being cocky the Portuguese really fancied their chances that day. After all, hadn't England just lost to Switzerland, and hadn't the Portuguese Army held the R.A.F. to a draw? And Portugal had insisted that the R.A.F. eleven was really an England team.

A slight argument held up the game. The Portuguese wanted to use their size 4 football, which is smaller than ours, and more like the size used by school teams in England. The R.A.F. team had played with the smaller ball, but the F.A. would not agree, and the game began with a full-sized ball. There was a terrific roar from some 60,000 fans, and then suddenly a depressing silence. In little more than ten seconds Tommy Lawton nodded the ball in the net with his head. You really could have heard a pin drop with the dreadful hush that followed.

When Portugal kicked-off again it was with the small ball. Laurie Scott was the first to notice it, but there was no protest from us, and in any case we were to slam in another nine goals. Make no mistake the Portuguese, although demoralized, were not so bad as the score suggests. If I may be permitted to say so England that day was one of the finest and most deadly football combinations in which I have had the honour to be included.

In seven minutes we were two up when Stan Mortensen crashed the ball past the unfortunate Portuguese goalkeeper, Azevedo. In eleven minutes Lawton let fly with a twenty-five yard drive, and England were leading 3—0. Tom Finney, settling down to the strange outside-left berth as though he had played in that position all his life, cracked in No. 4 after twenty-three minutes, starting with a remarkable dribble in his own half.

Even the shocked Portuguese crowd roared their approval of Finney's solo effort, but soon they turned their anger on the unhappy Azevedo, and began a chorus of shrill whistling which sounded like an express train approaching a tunnel. Soon afterwards Capela, the second-string goalkeeper came rushing on the field, and Azevedo left

"FOOTBALLER OF THE YEAR"

The author admires the bronze statuette presented to him as "Footballer of the Year" by the Football Writers Association on the eve of the Blackpool–Manchester United Cup Final

UNUSUAL PRECAUTION

Eddie Barks, the Mansfield Town outside left, is instructed to shadow Matthews in a Fifth Round Cup tie against Blackpool. Picture shows the Mansfield left winger standing marking Matthews. Blackpool won and went on to Wembley

in shame. This was against the pre-match agreement of substitutes, because Azevedo was not injured, but the referee's reply to a minor protest by England was a non-committal shrug.

And, furthermore, there was a second substitution a few minutes later when Cardozo, the right-back, was replaced by Vasco. In actual fact they could have changed the whole team, because nothing could have stopped the England machine on this sunny Sunday in May. In a few more minutes Lawton scored his third goal. So half-time arrived with England leading 5—0 to say nothing of what looked like two good goals by Lawton and Finney which were disallowed.

We were so confident and so much on top of Portugal that we continued the good work in the heat of the second half. It was the local team that began to tire, and I now found that Feliciano, the left-back, had given up hope, and it was an easy task to run round him. Mortensen soon cracked in a couple of goals, and Lawton scored his fourth. After this Mortensen got another which meant Stan and Tommy had shared eight goals between them. And even I came into the goal-scoring list just before the end when I tapped the ball past Capela to bring the England total to double figures. We had slammed Portugal 10—0, which I said earlier was quite a different Lisbon story compared with the R.A.F.'s visit.

But let me clear up one thing about Portuguese sportsmanship. The Portugal team did not turn up at the banquet that night, and were later suspended by the Portuguese F.A. Being a latin race the Portuguese are more temperamental than the British. Naturally, we would consider it poor sportsmanship not to turn up at a banquet because we were well beaten. But it was not so much poor sportsmanship as genuine shame that caused the Portuguese players to slip off to their homes, and I was glad when our own F.A. made a special request for the suspension on the team to be lifted.

Throughout the game the players showed wonderful sportsmanship. They were almost provoked into resorting to heated tactics by the manner in which we toyed with them, but tempers were kept, and there was not a vicious foul in the game.

CHAPTER XXVII

FOOTBALLER OF THE YEAR

My friends the Press. . . . We win at Hampden. . . . No banquet for Frank Swift. . . . A man with a plan. . . . Matches are won on the field and not in the stand.

ONE of the proudest moments of my life occurred on the eve of the 1947–48 Cup Final between Blackpool and Manchester United when I received a magnificent bronze statuette from the newly-formed Football Writers Association which honoured me with its vote "Footballer of the Year." My club colleague Mortensen was voted No. 2, and my friend Frank Swift No. 3. I say with all sincerity that I did not expect to win the vote of England's leading football writers, and I am sure I did not deserve it. However, the critics voted in my favour, and I shall always treasure the statuette with the other trophies football has provided me with.

Some of my best friends are among the football writers for whom I have the highest esteem. There are too many to name here, but I would emphasize that the football writers of England are of high integrity. They have been kind to me over the years, and yet whenever I have played badly they—some of them personal friends—have been the first to criticize me. That is why most footballers admire the reporters for their frankness, and I have yet to find the footballer who does not agree that the Soccer press is a good friend of the players.

The Football Writers formed their association during the 1947–48 season, and held their first dinner in London on the eve of the Cup Final. Many distinguished football and Fleet Street personalities attended. Invited along with me were the Blackpool chairman, Mr. Harry Evans, and our manager, Mr. Joe Smith. The ceremony of the presentation of the bronze statuette was broadcast. I have mentioned on another page that I am no after-dinner speaker, and it would certainly have been easier for me to have turned out before 100,000 football fans than to say a few words into the mike, and to my friends of the Press who had honoured me.

Fortunately, I know my limitations as a speaker, and, therefore, I don't make the mistake of talking too long, and from this aspect I am perhaps more popular as a speaker than I at first thought. I remember telling my listeners that sometimes they had written I could make a ball talk, and that certainly I wished I could have made the ball talk on my behalf on this occasion.

The football writers had a jolly and successful evening for their first big occasion, and I know there will be many more such evenings. Unfortunately, I had to leave early as I was making my first appearance in the Cup Final next day, and as Blackpool's headquarters were at Ascot I left with my chairman and manager for the drive to Ascot, and an early bed-time.

The next day meant everything to me. Blackpool had had one of its greatest seasons, and only two weeks earlier I had played in the England team that had beaten Scotland 2—0 at Hampden Park—a victory that meant the International Championship for England. All that was wanted now was the Cup for Blackpool and a Cup winner's medal—the one trophy in football that I have never managed to get my fingers on. But before I go on to the Cup Final let me say a few words about the Hampden game, and the cup-ties that preceded our trip to Wembley.

Victory at Hampden is always sweet for an England team—probably because of the pre-war bogy when a win against Scotland in the huge Hampden bowl always seemed to escape us. The England team gathered together a few days before the match, at Troon, under the eye of the F.A. team-manager, Mr. Walter Winterbottom. We had a few minor casualties that required treatment from trainer Jimmy Trotter. I had a slight bruise on my ankle. Mortensen had a sore throat and Lawton had severely grazed a knee as the result of a fall on the hard ground when playing for Notts County the previous Saturday.

Tommy was given daily penicillin treatment by Jimmy Trotter who blew the drug on to the injured knee. The improvement was rapid, and although Lawton wore a knee bandage when training on the Ayr United ground there was never any real doubt about his fitness or that of any other member of the England team. Scotland had managed to hold us to a 1—1 draw at Wembley the previous year when Billy Steel made his debut for Scotland, so we were particularly anxious to gain a victory this time, and particularly to make sure of the championship because Ireland were in a strong position if we tripped up at Hampden.

There were one or two changes in the England side. Harry Cockburn, the Manchester United left-half, and Stanley Pearson, the Manchester United inside-left, who had scored a hat-trick for his club against Derby County in one of the semi-finals of the Cup (strangely another Stanley scored a hat-trick in the other semi-final when Mortensen cracked three past the Spurs at Villa Park) were selected. I naturally was disappointed that my club colleague and captain, Harry Johnston, was omitted. Harry had been playing well behind Mortensen and myself this season, and not unnaturally, Stan and I were hoping that Blackpool's right triangle might be selected for England, but it was not to be. Scotland caused one big surprise by selecting Ian Black, the young Southampton goalkeeper.

There were the usual Hampden scenes when 135,000 fans cheered as Field Marshal Montgomery came on to the field and shook our hands. He spoke a few words to Tom Finney and Willie Thornton who both served in the Eighth Army and were members of the world-famous Desert Rats.

The teams lined up like this:

Scotland: Black (Southampton), Govan (Hibernian), Shaw, D. (Hibernian), Campbell (Morton), Young (Rangers), Macaulay, (Arsenal), Delaney (Manchester United), Combe (Hibernian), Thornton (Rangers), Steel (Derby County), Liddell (Liverpool).

England: Swift (Manchester City), Scott (Arsenal), Hardwick (Middlesbrough) (captain), Wright (Wolverhampton Wanderers), Franklin (Stoke City), Cockburn (Manchester United), Matthews, (Blackpool), Mortensen (Blackpool), Lawton (Notts County), Pearson (Manchester United), Finney (Preston North End).

It was not a great game, but England took their chances—one in each half—and deserved to win. Tom Finney scored quite a remarkable goal from fifteen yards out in the first half, and Mortensen scored our second goal in the sixty-fourth minute.

Frank Swift is not likely to forget this game. Big Frank, who along with my old Stoke colleague Neil Franklin, had outstanding moments in the defence—especially in the first quarter of an hour when with the Hampden Roar behind them the Scottish team had us pinned back in our own half. Big Frank was bundled into the back of the net by Liddell twenty minutes from the end. He was obviously hurt, but refused to quit because Hardwick, who normally would have deputized in goal, was also injured and was limping at outside-left, but he had to be assisted off the field at the finish. Once in the dressing-room an ambulance was called to take Swift off to hospital for an X-ray on his ribs which he feared were cracked. It meant no banquet for Frank that night. In fact, the hospital wanted to keep him there all night, but as Mrs. Swift had come to Glasgow for the match, the doctor agreed to let the England goalkeeper go back to his hotel, and rest in bed. Frank did this, and returned to Manchester next day, but after the long journey from Scotland collapsed on the station, and was taken home to bed.

We didn't think Big Frank would be fit enough to keep goal in time for the end of the season tour to Turin to play Italy, and then on to Switzerland for matches which were not classed as full internationals. Originally, the England party was to have two matches—

against Italy and Czechoslovakia at Prague, but the Czech match was cancelled after the Communist coup, and efforts for a substitute international against Spain at Madrid fell through owing to currency difficulties. So the F.A. decided on only one full international against Italy, and two representative games in Switzerland.

The good news for England was that Frank Swift was fit for the tour. The bad news that George Hardwick, the England skipper, was not fit. So Frank Swift was appointed captain for the first time. Not only the first time for Swift, but the first time a goalkeeper has captained England. Big Frank, of course, has been skipper of his club, Manchester City, for a couple of seasons.

With Hardwick unfit, Jack Howe, then a full-back with Derby County, received his first "cap" rather late in his career. Jack Aston, the Manchester United left-back, also chosen for the tour, but did not play against Italy. Incidentally, Howe is the first footballer wearing contact lenses to play for England.

The F.A. party rested at Stresa, which lies on the edge of beautiful Lake Maggiore, but as in 1939, we saw mostly heavy rain, which, of course, we took as a good omen for the conditions for the match. We were particularly anxious to beat Italy from a prestige point of view, knowing how seriously the Italians take themselves in games against England. I still had not forgotten the match at Highbury in 1934 or Milan in 1939. And, of course, the Italians are great ones for big bonuses in victory. We were told by friends in the know that the Italians were on £100 each if they beat us. In our case we were paid £20 each, win, lose or draw.

The atmosphere was tense in Turin. Fans were coming from all parts of Italy, and from quite a few spots in Europe. There was plenty of activity in the black market, and fantastic prices were offered for tickets.

There was still plenty of rain. In fact, there had been a thunderstorm the day before the match and another downpour before the game in which some of the 80,000 fans who began making their way to the ground six hours before the kick-off were drenched. It was an odd scene, thousands of men and women in brightly coloured shirts and blouses with thousands of black umbrellas. As the sun shone brilliantly before the kick-off the umbrellas finally served the purpose of protecting the fans from the sun!

The F.A. decided to rely on our most experienced team, apart, of course, from Jack Howe. However, although this was Jack's first international he is an experienced player in the League. The England team lined up this way: Swift (Manchester City) (captain), Scott (Arsenal), Howe (Derby County), Wright (Wolves), Franklin (Stoke City), Cockburn (Manchester United), Matthews (Blackpool), Mortensen (Blackpool), Lawton (Notts County), Mannion (Middlesbrough), Finney (Preston North End).

The Italian players were tucked away in a mountain hide-out, and the team was not announced until shortly before the game when Italy lined up: Bacigalupo, Ballarin, Eliani, Annovazzi, Parola, Grezar, Menti, Loich, Gabetto, Mazzola (captain), Carapellese.

From the kick-off the Italians descended upon the England defence as though they meant to over-run it, and believe me, they played some useful football, but our defence was magnificent with Frank Swift being even more inspired than ever as captain, and Howe combining perfectly with Scott. The Italians were playing their pretty football when we struck our first blow. The game was only four minutes old when Stan Mortensen beat the Italian goalkeeper. The ball had come to me. I managed to beat Eliani, and pushed the ball to Stan. In a flash he had cracked it in the net. Twenty minutes later we scored our No. 2. Neil Franklin had checked Gabetto, Italy's centre-forward, and with a neat pass sent me away. I passed to Mortensen, who made a fifty yard dribble at great speed. How he kept off Parola, I don't know, but he did, and also managed to give Tommy Lawton a good pass which Tommy put in the net.

Naturally, we were happy and confident with a two goal lead, although the skill of the Italians was excellent, and they had more of the play. However, it is goals that count, and in spite of all their pressure it was England who scored the next goal when half way through the second half Tom Finney banged in a Mannion pass. Two minutes later Finney completed a good job scoring from Mortensen's pass. So it was now 4—0, and the Italians had their tails down.

It was a good result for England, and we were a happy team that night. We felt we had done a good job of work for England, because never before had the prestige of English football been so high in Italy. It was altogether a fitting end to an undefeated season in international football.

And looking back to my club, Blackpool had had an exciting season for even though we had been beaten in the Cup Final we had at least reached Wembley. Oddly enough we reached the Final without having to face a First Division club until we met Manchester United. But we had tough opposition from the Second Division, Third Division and even outside the League—from the Cup giant-killers, Colchester United, who had so sensationally knocked out Huddersfield Town in the third round, and then went on to eliminate Bradford, who in the previous round had defeated Arsenal at Highbury.

Colchester United then had Ted Fenton, the old West Ham centre-half, as their player-manager. The team stayed at my hotel in Blackpool a few days prior to their Fifth round cup-tie against us. Joe Smith gave Fenton permission for his boys to train on the Blackpool ground—of course, at a different time from our own work-outs.

Ted was known as the " Man with a Plan." He claimed to have spotted defensive weaknesses in the Huddersfield Town and Bradford teams, and staged dress-rehearsals behind locked doors. He had great success, and was mobbed by 16,000 delighted Colchester fans when he steered his little club to the Fifth round. Although we won easily enough with a 5—1 score, I am convinced we would have had to fight pretty hard if we had had to visit the small Colchester ground. Although beaten Fenton's boys were not disgraced, and as the Mayor of Colchester put it, the local football team did more to put the town, famous for its oysters, on the map than any persons since Boadicea whipped the Romans at Colchester in A.D. 62!

I am personally not a great believer in placing too much faith in pre-arranged plans. Ted had a secret plan against us, but it misfired. The Fenton ambition of getting Colchester voted into the Football League succeeded, and was, no doubt, helped by the club's great run in the Cup.

Fenton has now returned to his old club, West Ham, as manager, and Jimmy Allen, the former Portsmouth and Aston Villa centre-half, took over at Colchester. In the 1951—52 season Blackpool were knocked out of the Cup in the Third round at West Ham. We had no grumble about the result, but I had to smile when I read a newspaper story that the " F " for Fenton Plan had worked again. Ted was quoted as saying he had spotted a weakness in our team, and that while he could not mention the name of the player, he gave his opposition player special instructions which worked accordingly. Every team, of course, has a weakness somewhere, but most big matches are won on the field—not in the stand.

In this particular cup-tie George Farm, one of the best goalkeepers in the country, made one of his rare mistakes, allowing the second goal to slip through his legs into the net. That was unplanned and unrehearsed. There's not much you can do about incidents like this.

CHAPTER XXVIII

COACHING—A MODERN CRAZE

Tommy Lawton, Joe Mercer, Freddie Steele, Neil Franklin, Raich Carter and myself were never coached.

WHILE I agree with a certan amount of coaching for school-boys, I must say I disagree with the craze that has hit the country for coaching, coaching, and more coaching. Whatever game you play, you need some teaching as a child, but I think it wrong when a boy with natural ability for a ball game is told he is doing things wrong, and that he must do everything according to the book.

Some of our greatest boxers, golfers, tennis players and athletes have done something that the orthodox coach would frown on, but these champions had something the coaches never possessed—natural ability.

Tommy Lawton, Joe Mercer, Freddie Steele, Neil Franklin, Raich Carter and myself are just a few players who didn't have any organized coaching, and I wouldn't say we suffered for this. Most of us practised like "mad." We picked up tricks by watching others and by playing as often as we could in any sort of matches. I would recommend to all young players the five-a-side games. Let them mix with more experienced players, and in this way they will quickly pick up positional sense.

Boys should, from the start, practise trapping and ball-control. But is it so necessary to trap the ball according to all the coaches? If a boy can get efficiency through unorthodox methods, I would allow him to continue with his own particular methods. A lad who is a born footballer will succeed, but I defy any coach to make a really good player out of a youngster who hasn't got what it takes.

Coaches should advise their pupils, but should not mould them so that they all look alike—just like a hundred cigarettes in a box. Last year I was asked to help a youngster. He had been coached as a winger. I took him on the pitch, and asked him to demonstrate his dribbling. He used both feet touching the ball from left to right toe, and back again. Now this method is good for practice, but not advisable in a match. I told the boy to dribble again, and warned him I would tackle him. He still insisted on using both feet and was very slow, and easy to beat. When dribbling use your natural foot. You will run faster, and have much better control of the ball.

I think tactical talks before a game are often overdone. Many a time I have read some story in one of the more sensational newspapers of how a match was won by a special pre-arranged plan. Although I have played in the match in question I confess I knew nothing about the plan until I read it in the paper. Perhaps somebody forgot to tell me about it!

We certainly don't overdo tactical talks at Blackpool. There are occasionally suggestions made, but Joe Smith has confidence in the common-sense of his team, and so long as everybody is doing their best Joe is usually happy.

So I will say no more about the coaches, but will recall a true story of a boxing instructor who was giving a youngster a lesson in the gym. The teacher was a pretty boxer with an orthodox straight left. His footwork was perfect, his punching was straight. His pupil was ten years younger, heavier and much stronger, but had little knowledge of the art of self-defence. He did, however, possess a natural ability to hit. The skilful instructor kept dancing in and out, and making the slugger miss, but in the second round, the younger fighter caught up with his dancing master, and with a right swing put him down for keeps.

When they brought the professor round, he grumbled: "Didn't I tell you to punch straight?"

That goes for Soccer coaches also.

CHAPTER XXIX

WHO SAID DREAMS COME TRUE?

Many a slip twixt Cup and lip . . . "This is it!" . . . smile from the King. . . . Well played, Manchester United! . . . Joe Smith and Matt Busby—two grand sportsmen

MY football story contains one big disappointment. I hoped to tell how Blackpool won the Cup, and how after eighteen years in football I had at last achieved my ambition of gaining a Cup winner's medal to pass down to my young son, Stanley. But who said dreams come true. This certainly was one occasion when a dream was shattered, but I am optimistic enough to believe that at Blackpool we have a team with sufficient footballing ability and fighting spirit to win the Cup before I retire.

Twenty minutes from the end of this 1947–48 Final I felt certain the Cup was ours. We had played good football and with a 2—1 lead I was confident that Manchester United would not overtake us. Then it happened. The slight slip that can change the fortune of a game. Jackie Morris, Manchester United's inside-right, who later joined Derby County, was going through outside the penalty box. Hugh Kelly, our left-half, went into a tackle, and for a few seconds both players became entangled. Referee C. J. Barrick (Northampton) blew his whistle, but I certainly was not sure against whom he had awarded the free kick. I am sure our defence must have been in the same doubt, because when Morris sprang a trick that I associate with Alex James he caught our defence unprepared, and Jack Rowley, the United centre-forward, headed in a great equalizing goal.

I am not squealing against Jackie Morris for taking a lightning kick before our defence realized what was happening. It is tactics like these that win games. In fact, one of our defenders should have kicked the ball away before Morris took his kick to give our defence a chance to get into position. This move is sometimes misinterpreted as unsportsmanlike, but it is legitimate, and really marks the experienced player. I emphasize, too, that neither myself nor any of my Blackpool colleagues have any kick against Mr. Barrick. The referee was in a good position, and I have since been told that he maintains Morris was pulled off the ball. I would, however, say on behalf of Hugh Kelly that he insists he did not pull Morris, and that when he heard the whistle he was certain that it was for a foul against Morris for cutting in front of him. Hugh said to me after the game; "All I did was to put my hand forward to save myself from tripping over Morris."

The game is now history. Blackpool did not complain at the time, and I am not complaining now, but I am emphasizing how an apparently unimportant incident can turn a game completely round. One minute Manchester were struggling. The next minute we had cracked, and the United were on top of us. Yet we still had one more chance to win the Cup twelve minutes from time with the score at 2—2. Stan Mortensen, who was chosen as centre-forward for this game, had roamed out to the right touch-line. An innocent looking ball came to Chilton, the Manchester centre-half, who misjudged the bounce. Stan was round him in a second, and was cutting in goalwards at a breakneck pace. True, he was shooting from a difficult angle, but knowing what Stan can do I said to myself: "This is it!" But the next second Mortensen had shot straight at Crompton, the United goalkeeper. It was certainly the end of Blackpool, because the ball was kicked down the other end to Anderson, the United right-half, who slipped the ball to Stan Pearson. Pearson made the perfect feint as though going to the right but actually swaying to the left, and sent in a great drive past Robinson. And five minutes from time Hugh Kelly, who had played really well, had more bad luck. A thirty yards drive from Anderson struck Hugh's head, and deflected past Robinson to give Manchester United a convincing 4—2 victory.

There is no blame attached to anybody. True, Mortensen might have won the game, but we have sufficient club-spirit to know that but for Mortensen's opportunism we might never have reached Wembley. In fact, we were almost beaten in the semi-final by 'Spurs, who were leading 1—0 with only three minutes to go when Mortensen dashed through to score the equalizer. In extra time he cracked in another couple for a hat-trick that gave us a 3—1 victory, and a pass to Wembley.

While on this subject I would like to pay special tribute to Joe Smith. How disappointed he must have been sitting on the touch-line. Twenty minutes from time it was Blackpool's Final, and then the crack-up, but Joe did not pass one word of rebuff in the dressing-room. Some managers would have allowed their disappointment to get the better of them, but Joe, who has two Cup winner's medals himself, is a good loser. This also applies to our chairman, Mr. Harry Evans, who took the defeat without murmuring. In fact, I am confident that had any outsider looked in at our dinner and dance in a West End hotel that night they could not have told that Blackpool had lost the Cup. It was one of the jolliest get-togethers I can recall, and only emphasized the wonderful club spirit we have at Blackpool.

We had had no pre-match plan—other than to play football at all costs. We were a team without nerves, and that applies to Johnny Crosland, the 24-year-old Blackpool accountant and part-time professional, who was brought in as a last minute choice at left-back to take the place of Ronnie Stuart, who failed to pass a fitness test. Considering Crosland, really a centre-half, had not played left-back in the first team, and had only made six previous League appearances he was one of the outstanding successes of the game. Johnny was an officer in the Fleet Air Arm, and won the D.S.O. He certainly showed he does not suffer with nerves when he accepted the roaring of a crowd of just under 100,000 and settled down to some great kicking—with both feet— and made a certain save from Jack Rowley in the first half when he headed out a ball from under the bar.

We all sympathized with Jimmy McIntosh, our regular centre-forward, who was left out of the Final as Joe Smith reckoned that the speed of Mortensen would upset Chilton—as, of course, it did. This gave a great chance to Alec Munro, who was Blackpool's outside-right when I was transferred from Stoke. Alec was brought in at inside-right, and played extremely well. And so did Walter

Rickett, our outside-left, who rose to the occasion, and was not the least bit overawed by that great back, Jack Carey. In fact, everything went according to plan, and even better than we had expected in the first half. Before the match Joe Smith had left us with these last words: " Play football, and do your best, lads. I shall not ask any more." Ten minutes before the kick-off we lined up alongside of opposite numbers of Manchester United, and each side led by their manager—Blackpool by Joe Smith, and Manchester United by Matt Busby—walked through the tunnel on to the green turf to be presented to His late Majesty King George VI. The crowd must have been surprised to see us appearing from the opposite end of the stadium to past Cup Finalists. Reason for this was that we were the first football teams to use the new Wembley dressing-rooms, built especially for the Olympic Games—and, of course, the new " lucky " dressing-room is the one used by the Manchester club.

King George came on to the pitch, and we were introduced to him by the captains, Jack Carey of Manchester, and Harry Johnston of Blackpool. For those whose memory needs a little jogging, the teams lined up like this: *Blackpool*: Robinson, Shimwell, Crosland, Johnston (captain), Hayward, Kelly, Matthews, Munro, Mortensen, Dick, Rickett. *Manchester United*: Crompton, Carey (captain), Aston, Anderson, Chilton, Cockburn, Delaney, Morris, Rowley, Pearson, Mitten.

The ball ran for us, and we could do little wrong. In fourteen minutes we were a goal up—the result of a penalty taken by Eddie Shimwell when Mortensen was brought down by Chilton. Stan had taken advantage of a slip by the Manchester United centre-half, and had made one of his great bursts through the middle. There was no stopping him. He was completely through. Chilton chased him hopelessly. Carey tried vainly to close in on him, but Stan was heading for goal. And then in the heat of the moment the desperate Chilton stuck out his foot and brought Mortensen down from behind. Referee Barrick came running up pointing immediately to the penalty spot. There were many present who say the trip was outside the area, and that Mortensen was going at such great speed that he shot yards into the area. The British Movietone pictures at the time suggested this, but few present did not agree that justice was done when Shimwell scored.

This was like a tonic to us, but inside fifteen minutes Jack Rowley had equalized when our defence was caught napping, and the Manchester centre-forward practically walked the ball into the empty net. But we were leading 2—1 ten minutes before half-time when we were awarded a free kick. I placed the kick in the goal mouth. Kelly headed it a few yards on, and Mortensen, turned in his stride, and cracked the ball in the net—as only Stan can. This marked a wonderful cup run for him. It meant he had scored in every cup-tie for Blackpool in the season—a total of ten goals.

We continued to play football in the second half, but things did not go so well. Yet I am sure we would have won but for that free kick against Hugh Kelly twenty minutes from the end which resulted in Rowley's equalizing goal. And still would have won if Mortensen had scored twelve minutes from time. But that is history now, and altogether we were satisfied. We had played football with great footballing opponents, and we had not disgraced ourselves.

When the final whistle blew, a sudden disappointment overcame me. It was like dreaming I had been left a million, and waking up to find that not all dreams come true. But we had no kicks. Soon we were shaking the Manchester United players by the hands.

A minute or two later we were lining up on the field discussing the crack-up as we just a little enviously watched Carey lead his triumphant men up to the royal box to receive the Cup and winners medals from the King. And then it was our turn. We followed up beaten, but not disgraced, and it was good to hear the cheers and condolences of " Well played, boys " by Blackpool fans. The King smiled with understanding as in turn he handed us the runners-up medals. I am sure he knew just how disappointed we were.

And then back to the dressing-room. No hard words from anyone. We had done our best and lost. What might have been wasn't and that was all there was to it. Joe Smith went into the Manchester United dressing-room to congratulate Matt Busby and the players on their success, and when we were dressed we did the same. I feel we owe a tribute to Manchester United for playing such fine football, and coming out on top after twice being behind. Some teams might have felt the urge to get stuck in, but Matt Busby had given similar instruction to his players as Joe Smith had to us—" Play football whatever happens " was Matt's request.

CHAPTER XXX

WEMBLEY AGAIN—BUT NO LUCK

You must have luck to win the Cup. . . . Joe Bacuzzi's goalkeeper's save was a passport to the semi-final. . . . Blackpool eleven minutes late for the replay. . . . Jackie Milburn's wonder goal. . . . No regrets for the past, and hopes for the future. . . . The real people.

WHEN our coach drove away from Wembley after our defeat by Manchester United we were satisfied with our showing, but were naturally disappointed, and not in the real spirits for celebration. Joe Smith's sportsmanship was superb, but we didn't take him really seriously when he consoled us thus: " Cheer up lads, it isn't the end of the world, and we'll be back at Wembley in the next couple of seasons anyway."

But Joe wasn't far out in his calculations. My old club, Stoke City, knocked us out in a replay at Blackpool the following season, and we reached the Sixth round in 1949–50 only to be beaten 2—1 by Liverpool at Anfield.

I missed this important match against Liverpool, having pulled a muscle in our Fifth round tie at Wolverhampton which was drawn. I missed the Wolves replay at Blackpool, which I remember as a really tough cup-tie. Eric Hayward was injured in the first twenty minutes, and Harry Johnston moved into the middle with Eric hobbling on the wing. To make matters worse for Blackpool, Billy Wardle, the left-winger, who later joined Birmingham City, was sent off the field just before half-time.

You can picture how Blackpool were up against it. We had only nine fit men throughout the second half, and I have seldom felt so anxious as I did watching this tie. Blackpool scored before the interval, so after the resumption it was a case of holding out the Wolves at all costs. We only had three fit forwards, and our hopes of increasing the lead were very small indeed. In fact, very often those three forwards came back into our penalty box to keep the Wolves out.

But how many times have you noticed that a team with only ten or even nine fit men fights with so much spirit that instead of being greatly handicapped they rise above themselves, and play better than with eleven fit players? This was certainly the experience of Blackpool this day, and Wolves just could not get through our defence, so that we lived to face Liverpool in the last round before the semi-final.

I had hoped to be fit, and Johnny Lynas worked hours on that pulled muscle, but on the Thursday before the match, I knew I could not pass a fitness test, and Albert Hobson again deputized. Blackpool were playing great stuff at this time, and our team-spirit was never higher. We were all confident we could beat Liverpool, and get into the semi-final—in spite of the fact that another non-starter was Eric Hayward.

Eric and I sat on the touch-line, and it was anybody's game all through. Eddie Shimwell had a good day against Bill Liddell, one of the most dangerous wingers in Britain. That was until the last quarter-of-an-hour. Liverpool then switched Liddell and Payne. With some eight minutes remaining, Payne took up a pass, and pushed the ball out to Liddell. Billy crashed through, and with one of his truly great shots scored the winning goal to beat us 2—1.

Liverpool reached the Final. They played their neighbours, Everton, in the semi-final at Maine-road, Manchester, and qualified for Wembley with a 2—0 win. Liverpool never found their true form in the Final, and were beaten 2—0 by Arsenal.

I can never repeat too often how great a part luck plays in any club's success—particularly in the Cup. I had left Anfield after Blackpool's Sixth round defeat, feeling that had the luck come our way on a couple of occasions we might easily have reached the semi-final. But luck goes round, and in the following season, 1950–51, we had plenty of good fortune in the Cup draw, and so reached Wembley for the second time in four years. Considering these were the only two occasions Blackpool had played in the Final in the club's history we were rather pleased with ourselves.

We were drawn away to Charlton Athletic in the Third round. I was a doubtful starter owing to a hip injury. I passed the test, but explained to our trainer that when I tried to get that extra yard it caused me pain, and actually prevented the extra spurt. It was arranged to give me a cocaine injection at half-time if I needed it. We went in 1—0 down. As my hip was causing me some disturbance, I had the injection which certainly deadened the pain.

We were lucky not to get knocked out, and sighed gratefully when three minutes from time, and losing 2—1, Mortensen equalized from a corner kick taken by myself. George Farm, our goalkeeper, was so relieved that he ran out of his goal and lapped the length of the pitch to pat Morty on the back. Both Charlton goals had been scored by their backs. The first a penalty taken by Charlie Revell, and the second when Peter Croker came into our goal area and headed in a corner kick.

Well, we had survived, but I had almost given up hope of taking part in the replay the following Wednesday. In addition to my strapped-up hip, I developed a cold on the Sunday afternoon, and the club doctor diagnosed 'flu. I was ordered to bed until Tuesday. I surprised Joe Smith by turning up at the ground on Wednesday morning, had a try-out on my injured hip which didn't cause me any bother, and was included in the team.

Charlton made unexpected changes in their team. Jimmy Seed, the manager, experimented with Frank Lock, the left-back, who had been out the previous Saturday with a cold. Lock was moved to outside-left with Charlie Revell, the wing-half, moving to left-back. It was a daring experiment, and did not come off. Lock went to his normal position in the defence during the second half, and Revell moved to centre-forward. With Mortensen scoring twice and Moodie also finding the net, we had a comfortable 3—0 passage into the fourth round when we were drawn at home to Stockport County. The plucky little Northern section club, managed by Andy Beattie, fought so hard that we were lucky to win 2—1.

Their defensive system was to switch the right-half and captain, McCulloch, to left-half to watch me. The left-back concentrated on the raids of Mortensen and Moodie down the middle. We were all pretty well held that afternoon, although I managed to slip the pass for Mortensen to score the goal. We were certainly relieved to hear the final whistle.

Don't ever think First Division clubs enjoy being drawn against Third Division sides in the Cup. Just think of Walsall, Bristol Rovers, Yeovil, Swindon, Leyton Orient, Southend United and others who have joined the large list of Cup giant-killers.

Blackpool's luck still held, and we were drawn at home to Mansfield Town in the Fifth round. This tie was of special interest to me, because my old Stoke City colleague, Freddie Steele, was then player-manager of Mansfield. Freddie and I had been great boys for tactics when we were at Stoke, and I reckoned he knew every trick I had. But in this particular game he made a big mistake. He instructed Eddie Barks, Mansfield's outside-left, to shadow me all the time. When I went into the Town's penalty-box, Barks walked beside me, and kept as close to me as my own shadow.

The result was Mansfield had only four forwards, and Eddie Shimwell, our right-back, often had time to dribble the ball down into the penalty-area. We led 2—0 at half-time. Naturally, I thought Mansfield would now go all-out on attack in a desperate effort to draw level, but Barks continued to shadow me till the final whistle. George Farm, Blackpool's goalkeeper, had his quietest afternoon of the season.

And so to the Sixth round with another home draw—this time against Fulham. Again the luck ran with us rather than against us. After four minutes Joe Bacuzzi, Fulham's right-back, made a goalkeeper's save from Harry Johnston's first-time shot, when he observed that Ian Black, his goalkeeper, had advanced out of his goal. Naturally, a penalty followed and Allan Brown crashed in what proved to be the only goal of the match, and a passport to the semi-final.

It was a tragedy from Fulham's view, because that Harry Johnston drive was going wide of the goal. Poor Joe Bacuzzi! He couldn't possibly have judged with his back to his own goal. All he knew was that the goalkeeper was out, and the ball was going goalwards. He confessed afterwards that the shot was too high for him to head, and that instinctively he handled as a last resort. Both Harry Johnston and several of Bacuzzi's own colleagues told him afterwards that the shot would have gone wide!

Jim Taylor, the Fulham centre-half, and captain had a great day, and played a major part in keeping us subdued. But for the bad luck of Bacuzzi we would have had to make the trip to London for the replay.

In the semi-final, we were drawn against Birmingham City at Maine road, Manchester. It was one of those tough cup-ties in which neither side managed to score. Oddly enough, the other semi-final between Newcastle United and Wolves also ended in a goalless draw at Hillborough, Sheffield.

Stan Mortensen injured his shoulder in the first half, but carried on, although in some pain. Our biggest let-off came two minutes from time when Stewart, the Birmingham winger went through and a fine drive struck the bar. We breathed again. The luck you need to get to Wembley had come our way because in the last five minutes the Birmingham forwards were raiding our goal almost non-stop, and it was a fine performance by our defence to hang on.

The replay was at Goodison Park. On the day of the match we took an early lunch at St. Anne's and left by coach in plenty of time, but we ran into such heavy traffic that we finally drove into Goodison Park less than ten minutes before we were due to kick off. Birmingham had arrived an hour earlier. It was a mad scramble to get ready. There were still thousands trying to get inside, and they must have been pleased we arrived late. When we hurried on to the field we were eleven minutes late, and London referee, Mr. A. Bond reported us to the Football Association. Mr. Bond, manager of a newsagent's shop, missed his train back to town, and had to wait in Liverpool until late in the evening. He travelled overnight in order to be at his shop for duty at five o'clock next morning.

We took Birmingham in this replay. Blackpool settled down immediately, and in four minutes Mortensen scored when Merrick could only half stop a drive. The greasy ball was, I think, over the line, but in any case, Perry made doubly sure cracking the ball into the back of the net from the rebound.

We scored again in the second half when Perry dashed through on his own after taking a pass from Brown. Birmingham, who never gave up fighting, hit back a minute later with a goal by Smith, but, thanks to some good work by George Farm, who was knocked out out earlier by an accidental kick on the head, we pulled through, and it was Wembley again. Was that elusive Cup Winners' medal to come my way at last?

But once more it was not to be. Newcastle United, who had beaten Wolves in the other semi-final replay, were, like Manchester United, worthy opponents, and worthy Cup winners.

Blackpool didn't undergo any special preparation. We took brine baths, played golf, and went about our normal training. We were really confident this time because, whereas Newcastle were going through a bad patch, we were bang in form. We were, in fact, in the running for the "double"—the Cup and League championship. We had a run of twenty games without defeat, and although we didn't bring it off either, we had a good season, finishing third with 50 points behind 'Spurs and Manchester United.

But our real set-back came when Allan Brown damaged a knee against Huddersfield. All the efforts of our trainer to get him fit for Wembley came to no avail. More bad luck followed when a week before the Final George McKnight was picked as inside-left against Sheffield Wednesday as a try-out for Wembley. He received a knee injury twenty minutes after the kick-off which ruled him out of the Cup Final team. So Bill Slater, the England amateur international, who later joined Brentford, was called in.

It was a disappointing Final for us. There was not much good football up to half-time, mainly because of Wembley nerves. We went in after a goalless first half realizing how much the first goal would mean to either side. Five minutes after the interval, Jackie Moodie pushed the ball through to me. I beat Bobbie Corbett, who later joined Middlesbrough, and cut along the line. I spotted Morty making a typical dash down the middle, and I quickly cut the ball back. It was too fast for him. He raced back, but stumbled, and George Robledo fastened on to the ball, and was away. George passed to Jackie Milburn, who ran through, drew Farm out of goal and scored. Yes, scored the vital first goal at Wembley. Two or three of our defenders protested that Milburn was off-side, but the referee, Mr. W. Ling (Cambridgeshire), immediately awarded a goal.

There was not any squealing from Blackpool at the time, and there certainly isn't any coming from me now, but I do want to say how easily it might have been Blackpool's first goal, had my pass to Morty come off. You remember how I explained a similar incident occurred in our Final against Manchester United which swung the game against us just when we were getting on top.

Five minutes later Milburn crashed in a dream goal from nearly thirty yards out to make it 2—0 and seal our fate in the Final. Ernie Taylor, now a Blackpool player, made the back-heel pass. Milburn came running in and hit a most spectacular goal with his left foot. A great goal for Wembley, but I wonder if Milburn hadn't already scored five minutes earlier whether he would have chanced such a long drive? Jackie is a good sportsman, and admitted afterwards: "My shot might have gone anywhere!"

True enough, but it is gambles like these that make Soccer such a thrilling and great game. He took a chance, and it came off, and so this match will be recalled as "The Milburn Final."

And so for the second time in four years we had just missed the boat. Joe Harvey, the Newcastle skipper, led his team to the Royal Box to collect the Cup, and Goalkeeper Fairbrother carried away the plinth. We followed Harry Johnston up for our consolation prizes—the runners-up medals.

Yet we were not downhearted back in the dressing-room. As against Manchester United, Joe Smith showed good sportsmanship. There was not one word of criticism against any member of the team. "You did your best, lads," said Joe, "and that's good enough for me."

After all we didn't have anything to be sorry about. We had at least reached Wembley twice, and that is something worth while.

My congratulations go to Newcastle and Joe Harvey who went to Wembley the following season—and again won the Cup, beating Arsenal—a great performance indeed, to win Soccer's most coveted prize in successive seasons.

What does the future hold for me? When I originally sat down to write *Feet First* I reckoned I had another five years of football left in me. I believe I still have five years to go, because I am as fit to-day as I was four years ago.

But whatever the future holds for me, I shall never look back with regret that I was once a member of that grand army of professional footballers who perform on the greatest platform the world of sport can offer, and whose efforts are watched by the most appreciative and most fair-minded spectators in the world. When the inevitable day comes, and my feet have lost the sparkle, I shall accept the inevitable, and will join the ghosts of former players, who now haunt the grandstands, the managerial offices, and the training quarters. I hope, too, to keep in touch with you, my readers and friends, through the columns of the *Sunday Express*.

As long as I have breath left in my body I must think, talk and live for Soccer. If ever I did quit the game I love I should age suddenly and fade away, because Soccer is life to me.

I have had lots of fun, travelled thousands of miles to strange lands. I have been fortunate enough to collect most of the honours football offers, and, what is more important, I have met real people and have made real friends in the Potteries, in Lancashire, and throughout Great Britain, and lands far beyond. I hope to share lots more fun with the supporters of Blackpool—and of other clubs, and, of course, with those of you who have derived some pleasure from my simple story. So I sign off wishing good luck, good health, fine weather and lots of goals for the little man of football, who week after week, year after year, stands on the terraces of grounds throughout this country and abroad, because he believes that Soccer is the finest and cleanest entertainment to be had. I am proud to have served him, because he is one of the real people.

THE COMPLETE STANLEY MATTHEWS INTERNATIONAL RECORD

1934–35				
Sept. 29, 1934	v.	Wales at Cardiff	England won	4—0
Nov. 14, 1934	v.	Italy at Highbury	England won	3—2
1935–36				
Dec. 4, 1935	v.	Germany at Tottenham	England won	3—0
1936–37				
April 17, 1937	v.	Scotland at Hampden	Scotland won	3—1
1937–38				
Nov. 17, 1937	v.	Wales at Middlesbrough	England won	2—1
Dec. 1, 1937	v.	Czechoslovakia at Tottenham ...	England won	5—4
April 9, 1938	v.	Scotland at Wembley	Scotland won	1—0
May 14, 1938	v.	Germany at Berlin	England won	6—3
May 21, 1938	v.	Switzerland at Zurich	Switzerland won	2—1
May 26, 1938	v.	France at Paris	England won	4—2
1938–39				
Nov. 16, 1938	v.	Ireland at Manchester (Old Trafford)	England won	7—0
Oct. 22, 1938	v.	Wales at Cardiff	Wales won	4—2
Oct. 26, 1938	v.	Rest of Europe at Highbury ...	England won	3—0
Nov. 9, 1938	v.	Norway at Newcastle	England won	4—0
April 15, 1939	v.	Scotland at Hampden	England won	2—1
May 13, 1939	v.	Italy at Milan	Draw	2—2
May 18, 1939	v.	Yugoslavia at Belgrade	Yugoslavia won	2—1
1939–40				
Nov. 11, 1939	v.	*Wales at Cardiff	Draw	1—1
Dec. 2, 1939	v.	*Scotland at Newcastle	England won	2—1
April 13, 1940	v.	*Wales at Wembley	Wales won	1—0
May 11, 1940	v.	*Scotland at Hampden	Draw	1—1
1940–41				
May 3, 1941	v.	*Scotland at Hampden	England won	3—1
1941–42				
Oct. 4, 1941	v.	*Scotland at Wembley	England won	2—0
Oct. 25, 1941	v.	*Wales at Birmingham	England won	2—1
Jan. 17, 1942	v.	*Scotland at Wembley	England won	3—0
April 18, 1942	v.	*Scotland at Hampden	Scotland won	5—4
1942–43				
Oct. 10, 1942	v.	*Scotland at Wembley	Draw	0—0
Oct. 24, 1942	v.	*Wales at Wolverhampton ...	Wales won	2—1
Feb. 27, 1943	v.	*Wales at Wembley	England won	5—3
April 17, 1943	v.	*Scotland at Hampden	England won	4—0
May 8, 1943	v.	*Wales at Cardiff	Draw	1—1
1943–44				
Sept. 25, 1943	v.	*Wales at Wembley	England won	8—3
Oct. 16, 1943	v.	*Scotland at Manchester (Maine Road)	England won	8—0
Feb. 19, 1944	v.	*Scotland at Wembley	England won	6—2
April 22, 1944	v.	*Scotland at Hampden	England won	3—2

1944–45				
Sept. 16, 1944	v.	*Wales at Liverpool (Anfield) ...	Draw	2—2
Oct. 14, 1944	v.	*Scotland at Wembley	England won	6—2
Feb. 3, 1945	v.	*Scotland at Birmingham (Villa Park)	England won	3—2
April 14, 1945	v.	*Scotland at Hampden	England won	6—1
May 5, 1945	v.	*Wales at Cardiff	England won	3—2
May 26, 1945	v.	*France at Wembley	Draw	2—2
1945–46				
Sept. 15, 1945	v.	*Ireland at Belfast	England won	1—0
Oct. 20, 1945	v.	*Wales at West Bromwich ...	Wales won	1—0
Jan. 19, 1945	v.	*Belgium at Wembley	England won	2—0
May 11, 1946	v.	*Switzerland at Stamford Bridge	England won	4—1
May 19, 1946	v.	*France at Paris	France won	2—1
1946–47				
Aug. 24, 1946	v.	*Scotland at Manchester	Draw	2—2
April 12, 1947	v.	Scotland at Wembley	Draw	1—1
May 10, 1947		*Great Britain v. Rest of Europe at Hampden	Britain won	6—1
May 18, 1947	v.	Switzerland at Zurich	England won	1—0
May 25, 1947	v.	Portugal at Lisbon	England won	10—0
1947–48				
Sept. 21, 1947	v.	Belgium at Brussels	England won	5—2
Oct. 18, 1947	v.	Wales at Cardiff	England won	3—0
Nov. 5, 1947	v.	Ireland at Liverpool (Goodison Park)	Draw	2—2
April 10, 1948	v.	Scotland at Hampden	England won	2—0
May 16, 1948	v.	Italy at Turin	England won	4—0
1948–49				
Sept. 26, 1948	v.	Denmark at Copenhagen ...	Draw	0—0
Oct. 9, 1948	v.	Ireland at Belfast	England won	6—2
Nov. 10, 1948	v.	Wales at Villa Park	England won	1—0
Dec. 2, 1948	v.	Switzerland at Highbury	England won	6—0
April 9, 1949	v.	Scotland at Wembley	Scotland won	3—1
1949–50				
July 2, 1950	v.	Spain (World Cup) at Rio ...	Spain won	1—0
Oct. 7, 1950	v.	Ireland at Belfast	England won	4—1
1950–51				
April 14, 1951	v.	Scotland at Wembley	Scotland won	3—2

*No Caps awarded